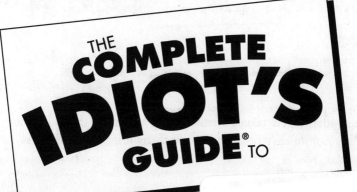

THE
COMPLETE
IDIOT'S
GUIDE® TO

D1320500

Trade Shows

by Linda Musgrove

ALPHA

A member of Penguin Group (USA) Inc.

This book is dedicated to my amazing support team! My husband Ralph,
my children Jeffrey and Rose, my parents Marge and George and
my dear friends Kathy, Jennifer, Barry, and Marty.

ALPHA BOOKS

Published by the Penguin Group

Penguin Group (USA) Inc., 375 Hudson Street, New York, New York 10014, USA

Penguin Group (Canada), 90 Eglinton Avenue East, Suite 700, Toronto, Ontario M4P 2Y3, Canada (a division of Pearson Penguin Canada Inc.)

Penguin Books Ltd., 80 Strand, London WC2R 0RL, England

Penguin Ireland, 25 St. Stephen's Green, Dublin 2, Ireland (a division of Penguin Books Ltd.)

Penguin Group (Australia), 250 Camberwell Road, Camberwell, Victoria 3124, Australia (a division of Pearson Australia Group Pty. Ltd.)

Penguin Books India Pvt. Ltd., 11 Community Centre, Panchsheel Park, New Delhi—110 017, India

Penguin Group (NZ), 67 Apollo Drive, Rosedale, North Shore, Auckland 1311, New Zealand (a division of Pearson New Zealand Ltd.)

Penguin Books (South Africa) (Pty.) Ltd., 24 Sturdee Avenue, Rosebank, Johannesburg 2196, South Africa

Penguin Books Ltd., Registered Offices: 80 Strand, London WC2R 0RL, England

International Standard Book Number: 978-1-59257-844-3
Library of Congress Catalog Card Number: 2008935067

11   10   09   8   7   6   5   4   3   2   1

Interpretation of the printing code: The rightmost number of the first series of numbers is the year of the book's printing; the rightmost number of the second series of numbers is the number of the book's printing. For example, a printing code of 09-1 shows that the first printing occurred in 2009.

Printed in the United States of America

Note: This publication contains the opinions and ideas of its author. It is intended to provide helpful and informative material on the subject matter covered. It is sold with the understanding that the author and publisher are not engaged in rendering professional services in the book. If the reader requires personal assistance or advice, a competent professional should be consulted.

The author and publisher specifically disclaim any responsibility for any liability, loss, or risk, personal or otherwise, which is incurred as a consequence, directly or indirectly, of the use and application of any of the contents of this book.

Publisher: *Marie Butler-Knight*
Editorial Director: *Mike Sanders*
Senior Managing Editor: *Billy Fields*
Senior Acquisitions Editor: *Paul Dinas*
Development Editor: *Ginny Bess Munroe*
Production Editor: *Kayla Dugger*

Copy Editor: *Amy Lepore*
Cartoonist: *Steve Barr*
Cover Designer: *William Thomas*
Book Designer: *Trina Wurst*
Indexer: *Celia McCoy*
Layout: *Chad Dressler*
Proofreader: *Mary Hunt*

Contents at a Glance

Contents

Introduction

There are literally thousands of trade shows every year in the United States alone. Many of these shows last multiple days, which means that on any given day there is a trade show going on somewhere in the country.

Trade shows are big business, and exhibiting in one is neither an easy nor low-budget undertaking. Unlike other marketing approaches, there is no easy and cheap way to try it out. When you decide to exhibit at a trade show, you are making a significant commitment of both time and financial resources, and you have to be in it to succeed. There is too much at stake to just see what happens.

The good news is that, with the right preparation and strategy, your investment in trade shows can easily pay off. There wouldn't be thousands of trade shows per year if the concept didn't work. David Letterman once said, "Next in importance to having a good aim is to recognize when to pull the trigger." This book provides the tools for a "good aim" to reach your key prospects.

Long before becoming a trade show consultant, I organized exhibits for businesses for many years. I learned many lessons the hard way, by trial and error and also by attending educational seminars about exhibiting and reading every piece of information I could find to increase the company's exhibiting a return on investment (ROI).

Given the size of the trade show industry and the cost involved in exhibiting, it is really surprising how many companies do so many things wrong. The primary reason is a lack of preparation, or simply not enough knowledge. As you will learn in this book, there is little to be left to chance, and detailed planning and research are a condition of success.

If you put in the necessary effort, there is no reason why trade show exhibiting shouldn't be the most profitable lead-generation source for your company.

When I was first approached about writing this book, I didn't hesitate even for a moment before agreeing to do it. I always felt there was a need for a book to help the busy marketing professional who one morning gets thrown into the role of trade show manager and has to make sense out of the many, often-overwhelming bits and pieces that make up trade show exhibiting.

This book will guide you through the various parts that lead to a successful and rewarding trade show experience. But keep in mind that the market, your customers, and your products will continue to evolve, and you will have to continuously fine-tune your exhibiting to get the good results you are looking for.

How to Use This Book

This book is divided into six parts to make your path to trade show exhibiting as easy and successful as possible. The first five parts cover the essentials, and the final part discusses specific shows and activities that may or may not apply to you.

Part 1, "Trade Show Basics" discusses trade show basics, what show types exist, and how to decide whether you should exhibit or not.

Part 2, "Planning: Space and Booth," discusses all the details involved in selecting and planning your trade show booth.

Part 3, "Planning: Marketing and Sales," explains the sales and marketing aspects of your trade show planning.

Part 4, "Final Prep and Showtime!" finally reaches the stage of actually exhibiting, and you will learn what to watch out for to make sure everything stays on track.

Part 5, "Postshow," covers all the activities that have to happen after the show to create sales and how to measure and report on the success of the show.

Part 6, "Special Types of Trade Shows and Activities," provides additional information on table top exhibiting, international exhibiting, and how to make the most of a visit as an attendee.

Appendix A contains a glossary to help you with definitions of terms you are not familiar with. Appendix B provides additional resources you can explore to learn even more about trade shows. Appendix C provides you with information about the CD that comes with this book.

This book also includes a CD to help you with your trade show preparation, and contains high-resolution images as well as a variety of templates that you can customize.

Extras

Throughout this book, you'll see notes called out in the text and in the margins. Be sure to pay attention to them. Here is what to look for:

def•i•ni•tion

This sidebar defines the vocabulary of trade shows to help you zip through the planning process.

Don't Do It!

This sidebar helps you avoid common pitfalls of exhibiting.

Show Smarts

This sidebar provides tips on how to get the most out of attending a trade show.

Budget Savers

This sidebar helps you learn where to save budget dollars.

Acknowledgments

I am grateful for the help and support of Paul Dinas, senior acquisitions editor at Alpha Books in New York, for asking me to write this book and all the invaluable help ever since.

I'd like to thank my husband, Ralph, for his valuable input on some of the content and for not being too grumpy about the many nights I had to work to meet the deadlines! Thank you to Maggie Santos for helping with anything thrown at her last minute. My two kids, Rose and Jeffrey, for their love and ongoing excitement for the book I was writing—the unlimited support my parents gave the kids and I by spoiling them all summer so I had time to write this book. I also have to thank my parents for teaching me valuable lessons by watching them while growing up, forming the professional I am today—how to be an entrepreneur by watching my dad run his own successful business and how to be a strong woman by watching my mom as she continuously held high positions in many associations she was a member of.

I am also very grateful to Kathy Watterson as my chief cheerleader and the rest of the Exhibit City News staff for their continued support. Last but not least, all of the industry contacts. To name a few: Ben Nazario from MC-2; Ron and Greg Abate from Expodepot.com; John Hogan from NMR Events; Frank Natoli from Global Events Management; and my colleague Susan Friedman, who is writing *The Complete Idiot's Guide to Target Marketing,* among many more!

Trademarks

All terms mentioned in this book that are known to be or are suspected of being trademarks or service marks have been appropriately capitalized. Alpha Books and Penguin Group (USA) Inc. cannot attest to the accuracy of this information. Use of a term in this book should not be regarded as affecting the validity of any trademark or service mark.

Trade Show Basics

Before you can even consider exhibiting at a trade show, you need to explore what options are out there. There are many different types of shows with distinct strengths and weaknesses.

This part takes a look at not only what types of trade shows you can possibly exhibit at but also where and how to find them. Once you have a list of possible candidates, you begin researching which ones are most likely to attract the kind of people you want to reach. The decision to exhibit or not exhibit is often a difficult one; there are so many variables to consider. One of the determining factors is cost, so we'll be looking at not only the many things you can spend money on but also how to create a professional trade show budget.

Chapter 1

What's a Trade Show? What Occurs?

In This Chapter

- ◆ Types of trade shows
- ◆ What occurs at trade shows
- ◆ Using the trade show's website as a planning tool
- ◆ Where to find trade show opportunities

Aside from making money for the show's producer, a trade show's primary purpose is to facilitate bringing buyers and sellers together for face-to-face interactions. Most exhibitors focus on attracting attendees to their booths to obtain qualified sales leads, but some exhibits are designed to inform attendees about upcoming products that are not yet available.

People attend trade shows for a variety of reasons, and many of these people are important decision makers. Some attendees come explicitly to visit the exhibit hall, evaluate vendors, and gather information for upcoming purchases. Others attend educational seminars and visit the exhibit hall only if time permits, just to see what is available for their market. Then there are those who do both. (Learn more about visiting trade shows as an attendee in Chapter 23.)

Both attendees and exhibitors often increase the value of attending a show by also attending networking events where they connect with peers, make new industry contacts, and build potential business opportunities. Networking events are also a great place to further develop any existing business relationships through face-to-face meetings and informal entertainment activities. (See Chapter 9 to learn more about networking.)

This chapter describes the variety of show types, venues, and typical events offered at trade shows, and it also provides ideas and guidance for the search of show listings.

Trade Show Categories

Trade shows are like shirts; they come in all sizes, colors, shapes, and forms. There is a trade show for every industry, in every size, and for every budget; the range is seemingly limitless. With a little bit of research, you will find a category that meets your specific exhibiting needs. Each category and the shows within that category have their own unique characteristics:

Sizes	Seminar offerings
Venues	Exhibit packages
Location	Networking events
Attendees	Industry variations

Show categories are introduced in order of price range, from least expensive to most expensive. Depending on the show, you may find exceptions to this rule.

Table Top Expos

In Chapter 22, you will learn more about table top exhibiting. These shows are inexpensive for exhibitors and rarely cost more than a few hundred dollars. They are usually offered by local business groups and chambers of commerce. Exhibitors and attendees are primarily a mixture of businesses from various local industries.

One of the exceptions to this is table top expos produced by a large single company in a specific industry. For example, the company may have a seminar event for which it invites several partners to show their complementing solutions in a table top exhibiting area.

Regional Trade Shows

These shows are budget-conscious, scaled-down versions of larger national trade shows. You will find mostly 10'×10' booths in these exhibit halls. Many of these shows offer seminars, but only a few offer networking events. Many regional shows are part of a nationwide show tour, with the organizers holding the same event at a variety of locations across the country. Nationwide exhibitors often participate in various regions, giving them access to otherwise untapped prospects. Expect attendees to come from within driving range of the event.

Vertical markets, niche markets, and regional chapters of larger associations dominate the orientation of this show type.

def•i•ni•tion

> **Vertical market** exhibitors have a product that serves a particular industry such as insurance, healthcare, legal, etc.
>
> **Niche market** exhibitors are from a subset of a larger industry. For example, the trade show industry is a subset of the marketing industry.

Virtual (Online) Trade Shows

After several years of existence, these events slowly started gaining popularity in the last year or two. On show dates, a virtual, interactive exhibit hall enables attendees to click on what they want to view—keynote speeches, educational seminars, booth spaces of interest, etc. Alerts let exhibitors know when attendees enter their virtual booth. Online chatting enables exhibitors to communicate with prospects and demonstrate their products, provide literature, and collect lead information for follow-up.

Because virtual trade shows can't duplicate the value of face-to-face interactions, these events won't replace traditional shows until Star Trek®–like holograms become possible, something I don't expect anytime soon.

National Trade Shows

National shows are dominated by *business-to-business (B2B) shows* produced for wide scopes of industries. Businesspeople from across the country travel to these shows as both exhibitors and attendees. A much wider assortment of activities is offered at national shows versus regional shows and typically includes the following:

◆ Substantial educational seminar programs

◆ Show-floor cocktail receptions

◆ Award presentations

◆ Exhibitor-planned parties

◆ Keynote speeches presented by business leaders, celebrities, comedians, and so on

Occasionally you will also find the following:

◆ Organized activities or tournaments, like golf and tennis

◆ A large event, such as renting out an amusement park at night, with shuttles provided and free admission and food

def•i•ni•tion

At **business-to-business (B2B) shows,** attendees and exhibitors are all businesspeople.

◆ Organized activities for spouses and children

Analyst-Produced Events

Several analyst firms produce high-caliber events with top-quality exhibitors, attendees, and presenters. Exhibitors are most often provided with booth space and the use of a preshow online planning tool that helps exhibitors request prearranged private boardroom appointments and prescheduled one-on-one meetings. Meetings occur with attendees in senior management levels such as directors, vice presidents, *C-level executives*, and industry analysts.

Educational seminars are geared toward the senior-level attendee. A variety of casual and formal networking events are provided. Occasionally these offerings include sports activities and other special events attractive to the respective audience.

def•i•ni•tion

A **C-level executive** is a top-ranking person. Here are some titles of C-level executives:

CEO: Chief Executive Officer

CIO: Chief Information Officer

COO: Chief Operations Officer

CCO: Chief Compliance Officer

CKO: Chief Knowledge Officer

CSO: Chief Security Officer

CFO: Chief Financial Officer

International Trade Shows

International trade shows can be huge in comparison to domestic shows. For example, CeBIT, a technology show held in Hannover, Germany, has 26 full-size exhibit halls. In 2008, the number of attendees was 495,000, not accounting for exhibitors. To put this into perspective, the U.S. Census Bureau's 2006 population estimate for the city of Miami, Florida, was 404,048 residents. Read Chapter 21 to learn more specific details about successful international exhibiting.

Trade Show Website

Most national and international shows provide a website that offers a "one-stop shop," locating all show details and forms for ordering services in one place. Whether you go to a show as an exhibitor or an attendee, it is always a good idea to spend some time reviewing the show's website. This helps you plan for the show.

Each show offers different levels of information; however, many shows have realized that exhibitor and attendee satisfaction levels rise with easy access to information. Fortunately, this leads to shows continuously improving their sites. The following table illustrates detailed information frequently available on trade show websites, separated by sections of the website.

Common Information on Trade Show Websites

Show Site Home Page	
Show dates	Who should attend
City and state	Who should exhibit
Facility	Links to defined sections
Show description	Preshow networking tool link
Show brochure	Registration

Attendee Section	
Exhibitor list	Conference sessions
Floor plan for booths	Registration
Exhibitor section	Exhibiting benefits
FAQ	Attendee demographics
Sponsorships	Show contacts
PR opportunities and help	Exhibitor testimonials
Expo hall hours	Exhibiting resources
Exhibitor kit	Register to exhibit
Update company profile	Booth staff registration
Deadlines	

Conference Program Section	
Seminar descriptions	Speakers
Keynote description	Speaker manual

Special Events Section	
Networking	Off-site events
Show-floor receptions	Friendly competitions

Press Section	
Press room hours	Press releases

Hotel/Travel/Transportation Section	
Airfare discounts	Show discounted hotels
Shuttle service	Hotel reservations
Parking	Driving directions

At-Show Items Provided to Exhibitors

There is no trade show governing authority. Industry associations offer suggested "best practices" for show producers to follow, but there are no actual requirements. Show producers set their own pricing and offerings, leading to vast differences among shows.

Here is an example of two basic show package offerings for comparable shows.

Show 1	Show 2
10'×10' booth space with pipe and drape	10'×10' booth space with pipe and drape
100-word description in show guide	50-word description in show guide
Company name and logo on show's website, linking to company website	Company name and logo on show's website, linking to company website
Electricity	
Table	
Chairs	
Standard carpet	
Sample Show Cost: $4,500	Sample Show Cost: $4,000

Don't Do It!

Key lesson: Don't choose a show based on price alone! All shows describe exhibitor packages differently; read the details thoroughly.

Example: A business new to exhibiting selects Show 2 (see the sample shows in the preceding table) based on price, thinking it is a better deal than Show 1. However, electricity, carpet, table, and chairs were not part of the exhibit package. They will have to order those items, and odds are the assumed savings are way less than the additional costs they will incur.

Where to Find Trade Show Opportunities

Many options are available for finding trade shows. Before beginning your search, see Chapter 2 to find out how to set goals for your company's exhibiting and the show information to collect for decision-making. Also read Chapter 12 to first make sure you know your exhibiting criteria and understand the needs of your key prospects. This preparation can save you considerable time during your search for a show that fits your needs.

The trade show search options that follow are listed in my preferred order for building a trade show list. I find this sequence to be most efficient, but you may want to adjust your show search order to suit your business's needs and work priorities. Chapter 2 describes how to create the template for organizing your show list, what key details to include, and how to determine the best shows for exhibits.

Trade Show Search Engines

The various search sites are the trade show equivalent to Google. Search options vary with each site, but most provide you with the capability to define details such as industry, month, city, state, and country, as well as to search for information on a specific show.

After searching within your parameters, a large number of show names will appear. Each listing and the information per show varies since it is entered by the show's producer. Most of these sites will provide you with show listings but will require a free registration to look at the show details.

Show Smarts _____

I used to find trade show search engines a great but frustrating resource. A good overview of the show is provided initially but not the show website or show contact information.

To get that information, you typically have to register with the site, which turns you into a lead for the show. I personally don't want to become a lead until I am sure the show is targeted. You can avoid this by using traditional search engines to find the show's website. Just enter the show name and a few other keywords. One or two keyword searches usually will find the show's website.

In the Chapter 1 section of the CD, you will be provided with links to many of the search options described here.

Traditional Search Engines

Since most trade show search engines primarily rely on show producers adding their shows to the site, results vary considerably on the various sites and never represent all shows that are produced.

Standard search engines such as Google can also be used to supplement your show search efforts. Enter keywords for the industry you want to exhibit in, plus the city and state; the results often list pages of show opportunities you may have otherwise missed. Try other keyword search variations as well. Another way to stay up-to-date on new events getting listed is to sign up for search alert e-mails such as Google Alerts. You will be automatically sent an e-mail every time one of your search terms is newly indexed on the Internet.

Industry Publications

Industry publications are commonly a good resource, listing industry-wide trade shows. Be aware, though, that these publications may focus only on promoting shows they produce themselves. Large media corporations that publish industry publications often produce several industry shows per year. On their home pages, look for links to resources, events, or trade shows. You can also look at the editorial calendar of those industry publications or media companies to find out which publications produce what shows and when they are held.

A good example of a high-tech industry publisher promoting their trade shows through their publications is Technology Marketing Corporation (TMC). This company produces several publications and trade shows. One of their most prevalent publications is Internet Telephony®, and they also produce the popular Internet Telephony Conference and Expo, which they promote in their publications.

Another example is a trade show industry publisher of a newspaper named *Exhibit City News.* This publisher does not produce their own trade show, but they promote lists of trade shows every month in their newspaper and on their website.

Industry Associations

Industry associations tend to organize at least one annual national show and frequent regional events. Listings can be found on their website's event page. Common words used for a national show vary and might include "expo," "trade show," "convention," or "conference." You can also find regional show listings by visiting event pages on the association's regional chapter sites. Many industry associations have subgroups that have their own websites, so don't just limit your search to the umbrella organization.

Show Smarts _____

Be conscious of the fact that not every show produced by an industry organization is a targeted one. Subgroups within the association, ones focused on your industry, tend to be better places to look for shows.

For example, you may have a technology product that targets the legal industry. The American Bar Association (ABA) has a technology group within the larger chapter. This group produces the National ABA TECHSHOW®, which attracts legal industry attendees specifically looking for technology products. This is an example of a targeted event from a subgroup of a chapter.

Convention Centers and Visitor Bureaus

Listings of shows within particular cities can usually be found on websites of convention centers and visitor bureaus. Besides the trade show calendars, you can benefit from additional resources available on these sites, particularly once you have selected a show. You can make practical use of information about the show's facility and the city's attractions, including great places to take prospects and current customers to dinner or to hold small events.

Newswire Websites

A few newswire companies offer trade show listings on their websites. One well-known company with a strong focus on trade shows is Business Wire®. When visiting its website, you can click on Events, where you will find show details listed by month, or you can sort by industry. If you click on the News link on the right-hand side, you will find additional show details such as exhibitor press releases for that show and a link to the show's website.

Chambers of Commerce

Chambers of commerce commonly offer table top expos for members' exhibits. If you belong to a chamber, the show information is typically announced at chamber events, through announcements and flyers, in monthly newsletters, and on its website. Most show attendees are other chamber members not exhibiting, as well as surrounding community and local businesses. Occasionally several local chambers collaborate to organize somewhat more regional events.

The Least You Need to Know

- ◆ There are many show categories with very different regional and industry reaches to consider.

- ◆ Attendees and exhibitors should spend quality time reviewing the show's website well in advance of the show to help plan their time at the show. The sites usually provide easy access to important show information.

- ◆ Review exhibit package details thoroughly before committing to a show, and call the show to clarify package details that are unclear to you.

◆ Make sure any show you choose targets the prospects you are looking for. Look for subgroups within industries for the most targeted events.

◆ Regional shows offer the ability to meet prospects that don't visit national events.

Chapter 2

To Exhibit or Not Exhibit

In This Chapter

◆ Setting goals and show search criteria

◆ Show data to collect

◆ Template guide for show list

◆ Deciding whether to exhibit

This chapter helps you determine whether you are ready to "pull the trigger" and begin exhibiting. You'll start by defining your exhibiting goals, which will help you search for targeted shows and collect the show data for decision making.

Finding the ideal trade show is a little bit like dating. You first need to figure out what you want, and then you need to know where to look. You know the perfect match is out there. With a little bit of searching, you will find many potential matches that come close to what you want. With a little more effort, though, you will find the perfect one ... trade show, that is!

Expectations, Goals, and Show Search Criteria

The overwhelming majority of businesses exhibiting at trade shows focus on obtaining sales leads. But that is not the only possible reason to exhibit. Other reasons include maintaining current business, increasing industry exposure, and making media contacts. You have to be clear about what you are trying to achieve with your exhibit. Answer these questions when establishing what you are trying to achieve:

◆ Which initial goal(s) is most important to you: new business (leads), maintaining business relationships, creating industry exposure, or meeting media contacts?

◆ What key industries should you exhibit in?

◆ What show types should you exhibit in?

◆ Who are the key prospects in each industry?

Show Smarts

Depending on your market, you should also take into account what shows your competitors exhibit at. Sometimes having a competitor at the same show can be a big plus because it creates more awareness for your product type; this is often the case if you are offering something innovative.

On the other hand, if you are competing with a market leader or a bigger company that has roughly the same offerings that you do, going to a different show where you can be the only fish in your industry pond can be more important.

New Business (Leads)

If your business's goal is supplying your sales force with qualified leads, find targeted shows with large volumes of key prospects. The better defined your target, the easier this is going to be. See Chapter 12 for more information about defining and reaching targeted prospects.

Most shows claim they are the perfect place to get leads. A show that is serious about offering good lead-gathering opportunities, though, offers free or paid attendee lists, exhibit hall receptions, and a variety of networking events. In addition, preshow networking tools, which help to arrange at-show meetings, are becoming increasingly common offerings.

Don't Do It!

Poor show selection, unqualified leads, or not attracting key prospects to the booth creates lost budget dollars, little to no sales, wasted sales team productivity, and unmet sales goals.

After finding targeted shows with qualifying key prospects, make sure you learn and apply the various strategies spread throughout this book to get those qualified prospects into your booth. Lead quality is imperative to a successful and speedy sales cycle, leading to a more productive sales team and increased company revenue.

Maintain Current Business

Exhibiting at trade shows to maintain current business is probably the easiest goal of all. Ask your most important customers what shows they attend. Have their account manager call them directly and just ask. If you are in an industry with fewer personal sales contacts, you will have to resort to some type of survey. Send an e-mail or postal mailing. If you can, offer some type of incentive for every customer who replies with his or her show attendance lists.

After you receive the show names, you have a ready-to-go list of shows to evaluate. If only a show name was provided, find a link to the show's site by searching trade show search engines and traditional search engines. Review the show's site, obtain show data, and evaluate the individual show opportunities. The primary component that these shows must have is a large number of networking and socializing opportunities.

If your primary objective is maintaining current business, consider visiting the show as an attendee instead of as an exhibitor. You can save a considerable amount of budget dollars.

Spend time with customers in formal business meetings and informal dinners. Also visit local activities of interest to them. Your focus is on growing the business relationship. People want to do business with friends, so these relationship-building activities will lead to valuable sales opportunities. Remember, when visiting as an attendee, it's important for these shows to have large numbers of networking and socializing opportunities.

Industry Exposure

If your business's primary goal is to further industry recognition by branding and building your image within the industry, look for shows that offer a great deal of advertising opportunities at reasonable costs. Sponsoring a networking event, contributing to event kits, or having your name printed on the event hotel's key cards can be great ways of getting your name noticed.

Other examples are preshow e-mails and postal mailers, show floor and outdoor signage, show guide ads, show daily ads, prominent logo placement on the show's website, and logo placement on show lanyards.

Show Smarts

It's often a good idea to call the event producers directly about media opportunities. Sometimes you get special insider tips. Frequently, when a show is associated with a publication, a good show sales rep will arrange meetings with the publication's reporters as part of an incentive for you to exhibit at the show.

Media Contacts

As an exhibitor, you should always have public relations (PR) initiatives for every show. (You'll learn more about PR in Chapter 11.) However, you should only define this as a primary goal when you are going to be making an important new or improved product announcement.

When you evaluate possible shows for this goal, remember that the highest concentration of media attendees tends to be at the larger, national shows. Other things to look for are spaces on the show's website for exhibitor press releases, preshow networking portals, preshow availability of the press list with contact information to arrange meetings, an at-show press room to put press kits, and press conference facilities.

Show Smarts

A PR firm active in your industry will typically know available media opportunities—whom to contact and how to make appropriate arrangements. When managing public relations activities yourself, you will achieve a much higher rate of success in reaching media contacts and achieving public relations goals if you do advance research of the media opportunities being offered by the trade show. Don't just rely on media opportunities being listed in show materials; call the show to ask about the most current and detailed information.

Show Prospectus and Show Audits

After you have outlined your goals and are ready to start your show search, always obtain the show prospectus. Show information and attendee data provided in the prospectus will vary in detail and accuracy, but in most cases it will have facts and figures about attendee profiles, titles, purchasing roles, budgets, sales volume, and geographic location.

A show prospectus may also include booth package information and a list of marketing opportunities. Most of the time, you can easily download this information directly from the show's website. Typically you will reach this information from a link to an exhibitor information area of the website designated as "exhibitors," "exhibiting," or something similar. When analyzing the data, keep in mind that the show prospectus is a sales and marketing tool of the show's producer.

Show Audit

Always ask if a show audit of the previous year's show is available. The types of facts and figures provided are very similar to those in the show prospectus, but show audits are verified by a third party, confirming attendee data accuracy by monitoring the show registration process and following up with attendees postshow.

BPA Worldwide; Exhibit Surveys, Inc.; and Veris Consulting, LLC are the only audit companies certified by the Exhibition and Event Industry Audit Council (EEIAC). As a cautionary measure, research other audit companies carefully before relying on the data provided. Don't be surprised if smaller shows don't offer a show audit; national shows and other shows with larger budgets are the ones commonly offering them.

Verifying Show Data

Something you should do in any case, but certainly if there is no third-party show audit available, is solicit information from exhibitors of the previous year's show. Select a few companies from your same industry or companies that target similar prospects. Simply call and ask to speak with their show manager. Ask about their exhibiting experience and whether it was worthwhile to exhibit there. The following are some sample questions to ask. You can add additional questions specific to your needs.

- Did you feel the attendees fit the show's description? Can you please explain?

- Was the show turnout good? Can you please explain?

- Would you exhibit there again? Can you please explain?

Another good source of information about the show is previous attendees. A reputable show will be willing to provide you with a small sample of previous attendees. Call several of them to ask about their impression of the show. The following are a few sample questions to ask. You can customize questions to your business needs.

- What were your reasons for attending? Did the show meet your attendance goals?

- Do you plan to attend again?

- What contributing factors make you want to attend again (or not)?

Don't Do It!

Most show managers are happy to help a colleague by answering questions about a show experience. Stay in touch if you hit it off with someone. You may become great resources for each other!

Also beware of the clever competitor show manager who befriends you and starts gathering competitive data from you! Show a sales or marketing manager the list of show managers you plan to call. He or she can verify whether a competitor is on that list or not.

Show Promotion Plan

Another item worth researching is the show producer's plan for the promotion of the show. This typically is not found on the show's website. A reputable show producer has developed detailed plans to reach and attract a well-defined audience and is willing to share that plan with potential exhibitors. At a minimum, any such plan should contain most or all of the following items:

- Defined target audience and how they will be reached
- An outline of print advertisements, including the publications they will run in, with publication distribution numbers
- Direct mail and e-mail campaigns—the number planned and to whom they will be distributed
- Press releases—topics, distribution schedule, distribution outlets, and other areas of placement
- Online advertising—list of websites, sizes of ads, and advertisement schedules
- Radio or TV coverage planned

If the show is not willing to share its plans with you, consider that a red flag because it almost certainly means it has something to hide. It might simply be that the producers are behind on their planning, but it could also be a sign of a greater problem such as disorganization, lack of planning, and lack of preparation for the overall show.

Show Smarts _____

Understanding the show promotion plan can be helpful in deciding where to spend your promotional dollars. For example, a small
"Come see [your company name] at [your booth #] at [enter show
name, city, convention facility] with [a list of your benefits]" ad has a
greater chance of success in a publication that already contains advertising for that show than being on its own in another publication.

Organizing Show Information

Whether you have been doing this for years or are just starting out,
having an organization strategy increases your productivity tremen-
dously.

Throughout this book you will learn organization strategies. This
specific information will prepare you for organizing the master show
list, selected shows, and show data. To keep yourself organized for the
upcoming task of listing potential shows, do yourself a favor and set
these folders up on your computer first. The following tables should
help you with this task.

Folders and Subfolders to Create on Your Computer

Folder Type and Name	Folder Location on Computer
Main folder: Trade Shows	Documents folder
Subfolder: Year (Ex: 2008)	Trade Shows folder
Subfolder: Shows for Consideration	Year (Ex: 2008) folder
Subfolder: Folder by Show Name	Shows for Consideration folder
Subfolder: Show Selections	Year (Ex: 2008) folder

Where Trade Show Information Is Placed

Name of Information	Folder Location
Master show list	Shows for Consideration folder
Show data (prospectus/audit)	Folder by show name
Show selection list	Show Selections folder

List Potential Shows

Applying the selected criteria and knowledge gained earlier, it is now time to create a master list. To be complete and efficient, your initial master list should contain all potential shows you are considering. Keep this master list available and add shows when doing routine show searches, something you should do at least once per quarter.

Create a separate list for the shows you choose to exhibit at; have one show selection list per calendar or fiscal year. Simply paste the information from the master list into your new show selection list. You can do this by either adding a new worksheet or creating an entirely new spreadsheet.

A Template Containing Shows and Key Details

Based on my own experience and having tried many different methods, I have personally found Microsoft Excel to be the easiest tool to use for creating show lists. It enables quick sorting of columns to view show details in order of preference. For example, you can sort columns to view shows by cost, date, industry, city, and so on.

The CD has a ready-to-use Microsoft Excel template for creating your show lists. If you prefer a different method, the following is the key information you need to gather during your collection of show details:

- ◆ Show name for consideration
- ◆ Industry
- ◆ Show goal
- ◆ Key prospect type
- ◆ Show website
- ◆ Show month
- ◆ Show dates
- ◆ Year
- ◆ City

- State

- Salesperson territory (if applicable)

- Booth size (the size your business is considering)

- Show package cost (the show package your business is considering)

- Notes (about your opinion of the show)

- Hyperlink to show prospectus/audit file

Show Smarts

Adding a hyperlink from the show list template directly to the folder containing the show prospectus and show audit will give you faster access to show data, which speeds the show review and selection process.

You fill find a template containing shows and key details in Chapter 2 on the CD.

Selecting the Right Show

Once your show list has been created, the next step is to review the list and show data. Careful consideration and initial show analysis has already earned each show a place on the master list. Create a new list to copy and paste the shows expected to produce the highest *return on investment (ROI)*, *return on objectives (ROO)*, and sales after a more thorough analysis of the show data is completed.

After you have your data together, hold a meeting to discuss the show findings. Depending on your company, this meeting may be with the sales and marketing department heads, a member of management, the owner directly, or possibly all three. Use this meeting to review show details and make final show selections. Make sure to bring the following items to the meeting: the master show list, show data, and goals by industry. If you have access to a projector, use it to show your various lists. If your show list was created in Microsoft Excel, it will be easier to make changes or sort the list differently during the meeting. Doing this not only helps save some trees, it also makes your meeting faster and more efficient.

def•i•ni•tion

Return on investment (ROI) is quantified by comparing the total show investment against the sales generated from the event.

Return on objectives (ROO) is an analysis of the return gained from show objectives that are not necessarily sales related, such as meetings with reporters, awards won, etc.

These definitions are common in the business world; the definitions provided here are to show how they relate to trade show exhibiting.

Selecting Shows to Exhibit At

To help you narrow down the master list, you should create a new list template to place the final selection of shows to exhibit at. For each show on the master list, you will need to review the show data against your goals and provide answers to the following questions to determine the viability of each show:

◆ What initial goals does this show meet?

◆ What key prospects attend this show, and what is their purchasing authority?

◆ Will you have the resources for effectively planning and exhibiting at the time of year the show is scheduled to be held?

◆ Do you have the budget for all related expenses? (Learn more about budget planning in Chapter 3.)

◆ Can your sales team manage the show leads acquired at that time of year?

◆ Are there other conflicting company events?

◆ Are there high concentrations of competitors exhibiting?

◆ Are the competitors too large or too well positioned to compete against?

Don't Do It!

Don't sign the exhibitor contract and make your payment commitment before reading Chapter 3, which is about budgeting. There are many exhibiting-related costs that reach far beyond the initial exhibit package costs that need to be taken into consideration.

Chapter 2 of the CD will provide you with questions to ask when selecting shows at which to exhibit.

The Least You Need to Know

- For each show, obtain a show prospectus and, if available, a show audit from the previous year to review show data as part of your selection process.

- Before searching for shows to exhibit at, set goals, define industries, and list key prospects you are looking to reach for each type of show.

- Start with a master show list template that gets updated quarterly when you search for shows to exhibit at. Create a separate list narrowed down to only the shows you will be exhibiting at.

- Verify show data by calling several show managers that have exhibited at this show before. Also ask show management for several attendees' contact information to speak with about the show.

- Organization in trade show planning is essential. Before starting a show search, create folders on your computer to manage the information you collect, making them easily accessible whenever needed.

- Make sure that the exhibiting budget is available, enough resources are available to effectively plan and exhibit at the show, the sales team can handle leads at the show's time of year, and there is a low concentration of competitors.

Chapter 3

The Costs of Exhibiting

In This Chapter

- ◆ Learn how to create an effective trade show budget
- ◆ Identify the items that need to be part of your budget
- ◆ Distinguish between budgets for ROI calculations and budgets for cash flow
- ◆ Use your budget plan to track estimated and actual costs
- ◆ Prepare to identify areas for future cost savings

I feel like a used car or timeshare salesperson right now. You've read the first two chapters; learned the value and benefits of exhibiting; and determined where to find shows, how to set goals, and how to create a master show list. You've even narrowed down the master list to the most targeted shows for your business. This chapter introduces the many other items to factor into the costs of exhibiting.

Unlike many other marketing areas, there are no trial versions to cheaply test trade show exhibiting, and the basic cost is not low. Subsequently, it is important for you to understand the opportunities and ROI potential so that you are able to put the cost items into the right context.

John F. Kennedy once said, "There are risks and costs to a program of action. But they are far less than the long-range risks and costs of comfortable inaction." This also applies to trade show exhibiting. The initial expenditure is fairly high, but so can be the rewards as well as the competitive risk of not exhibiting at all.

This chapter describes trade show budgeting in detail and shows you how to create a budget template to help estimate the costs per show and then track the actual costs.

Trade Show Organization and Budgeting

Organization is a key component of successful trade show exhibiting. Maybe you're the type who prefers the sticky-note method to plan and remember deadlines, but that strategy won't work for creating a successful trade show exhibit. There are many variables to consider, and the available colors for sticky notes are just way too limited.

 The budget template is just one of the many valuable tools on the CD designed to help you learn organizational strategies for planning your shows.

If you dislike spreadsheets and other various planning tools, keep in mind that learning how to use them is far less painful than explaining to management why you exceeded your budget, missed deadlines, and did not meet anticipated goals. It may take a little getting used to, but planning tools and organization are lifesavers for trade show managers. Having all your information organized and easily accessible will keep you sane.

Determine Costs: Create a Budget

If being strict with numbers and working with budgets was your thing, you probably would have chosen a career in accounting rather than trade show marketing. However, without a budget, it is easy to get carried away and spend a lot more than anticipated on the many details and expenses involved in planning a trade show. There are many creative ways to reach key prospects and to spend money on a trade show; that's why budgeting is essential.

Budgeting involves allocating a range of available funds and creating a guide as to how to spend them. Advertising, promotional items, direct mailings, and a new display are all examples of great marketing items for a trade show, but they all come at a cost. Your budget will be a guide to help you plan fundable activities that meet your goals for each show.

Items to Budget For

Although there are only 11 key categories to budget for, there are numerous expense items within each category that will differ by show type, show size, and whether they need to be purchased or rented. When you create your budget, you can use the sample items listed in the following table as a guide and then customize and define the specific items for your business's budget. The table provides you with typical cost items you can use to plan for your budgeting of each show.

Eleven Categories to Budget for with Examples

Exhibit Package	
Booth space cost	Exhibitor badges
Lead Capture	
Lead capture device	Lead form printing
Display Properties	
Graphic design	Display
Refurbishing display	Shipping of purchase
Accessories	Insurance for display and shipping
Marketing	
Collateral	Promotional items
Advertising	Direct-mail printing
Direct-mail postage	Mailing list rental
E-mail list rental	Presentation talent
Sponsorships	Host networking event
Hospitality room(s)	Business cards
Meeting rooms	

Supplies

Track in supply spreadsheet

Miscellaneous/Contingency

Miscellaneous/contingency	Show-required insurance

Public Relations

Press conference	Press kits
Press release distribution	Press meetings (food and drink)
Press-only private event	Other

Personnel Expenses

Staff attire	Staff training
Preshow staff dinner	

Travel

Lodging	Airfare
Car/transportation	Meals

Show Services

Attendee badges	AV/computer rental
Booth cleaning	Carpet and padding rental
Security	Electric rental
Exhibit design/rental	Extra exhibitor badges
Floral rental	Forklift rental
Freight	Furniture rental
Internet rental	Labor
Phone rental	Material handling/drayage
Photography	Security
Storage (at show)	

Shipping

Inbound shipping	Outbound shipping
Customs	Warehouse services

Tracking Costs in the Budget Spreadsheet

For each of the 11 key budget areas, you need to list actual budget items specific to your company, along with estimated costs and actual costs. You also need to track the paid and unpaid status of these items as well as other details.

The following list explains the various columns of the spreadsheet and how to use them.

- **Item:** These are the items to budget for within each of the 11 key categories.

- **Estimated costs:** For each item, you will need a cost estimate. (The next section is a helpful guide.) You can also call vendors and get an estimate of what each item will cost you.

- **Variance %:** Figure a percentage that the estimate might be "off" by. You will develop a good sense for this over time. Ten percent is a good starting point in most cases.

- **Notes:** Any notes or reminders you want to include.

- **Variance low:** Based on the estimated costs and the variance percentage you listed, this column will show the least amount you expect to pay for a particular item.

- **Variance high:** Based on the estimated costs and the variance percentage you listed, this column will show the highest amount you expect to pay for a particular item.

- **Final actual costs:** Once you know the final costs paid per item, add the cost to this column.

- **Internal P.O. #:** If your business requires a purchase order for each item, list the purchase order number (P.O. #) in this column. If this is not applicable, this row can be deleted from the budget spreadsheet entirely.

- **Invoice #:** For most items purchased or rented, the vendor will send you an invoice. This is where you can track the invoice numbers for easy reference, which will help when dealing with vendors or your accounting department.

♦ **Payment method:** Describe how each item was paid for, typically by credit card or check. Vendors asking to be paid in cash should be scrutinized carefully. This also helps you work with your accounting department more efficiently.

♦ **Date paid:** Enter the exact date items were paid for. This is another area that helps you work with your accounting department efficiently.

Show Smarts

Paper items can be lost or misplaced. Losing a paper item while planning a show can create major chaos for you.

If you have a scanner, scan paper items such as purchase orders and invoices to the specific show folder on your computer. Some networked copiers even allow you to scan multiple items at once and save the documents in a single PDF file.

Estimated Costs

Newer exhibitors find estimating costs per show to be more challenging than seasoned veterans (who have a feel for costs already) do. To grasp a general cost estimate, the industry publication *Tradeshow Week* recommends that you "figure your total trade show cost will be three times the cost of the exhibit space." In general, I agree with that assessment, but this varies quite a bit depending on the location of the show.

The following statistics are from the Center for Exhibition Industry Research report "How the Exhibit Dollar is Spent," which was created using data from the Exhibit Designers and Producers Association (EDPA), the Trade Show Exhibitors Association (TSEA), and the Center for Exhibition Industry Research (CEIT). These numbers can be used as a general guide to determine average percentages of your trade show budget allocation. Keep in mind that this data will vary for future shows once you have purchased big-ticket items such as your display. This data is based on a four-year average of Trade Show Exhibitors Association (TSEA) data.

- Exhibit space: 31%

- Exhibit design: 11.2%

- Show services: 20.3%

- Shipping: 10.8%

- Travel and entertainment: 15.3%

- Promotion: 7.5%

- Other (miscellaneous/contingency): 4.9%

Budgeting for ROI

Many items are used for more than one show. These costs should not be applied to only one show's budget; rather, they should be spread across several show budgets. This is important to accurately evaluate and measure the financial performance of shows.

Let's use the following table as an example. First, estimate how many shows will use the same display over the lifetime of the display. Divide the total cost of the display and accessories by the number of shows at which you will use the display. This, then, is the amount that should be applied to each show's budget for the life of that display. When a new display is purchased, apply the costs to the budget in the same manner. This same formula should be used for each item that will be used at several shows.

Example of Spreading the Cost of an Item

Trade show display cost:	$5,575.00
Display usage at trade shows:	12 times
Divide costs:	$5,575.00 ÷ 12
Display costs for next 12 budgets:	$464.58

Working With Your Accounting Department

Often when you take on the role of full-time trade show manager, you are essentially turned into a "department of one" that will work closely with other departments. Because most of this book is dedicated to working closely with sales and marketing, you should also think about working closely with the finance department. Of course, the possibility of this working relationship depends on the structure of your company and whether such a cross-functional relationship is permitted or encouraged. Typically, in smaller organizations, it is a good idea to plan a meeting with the appropriate people in the finance department to introduce yourself (if you haven't already) and discuss the new role that trade shows will play in creating leads for the sales team and revenue for the company. Be prepared to discuss the initial approved budget you have been given for the year and how you have allotted the budget dollars per show in the ROI budgeting spreadsheets. Ask for the finance department's advice on the next steps you should take to pay for budgeted items.

Budgeting for Cash-Flow Purposes

It is important to distinguish between budgeting for ROI purposes and for cash-flow purposes. You may be more interested in ROI budgeting, but the accounting department is probably more interested in budgeting for cash flow.

A cash-flow budget has the same expenditure items as your overall budget, but they are listed in the order they have to be paid. Some items might be split up and appear twice. For example, you may have to pay 50 percent of your booth package at the time of registration and the remaining 50 percent at least two weeks before the show. Also, any *assets*, such as your booth display, that *depreciate* over time will have to be recorded in the cash-flow budget when they have to be paid. As a result, a cash-flow budget can look very different from an ROI budget. So if cash flow is an issue for your organization, make sure you create a cash-flow budget based on that show's monthly spending as it is expected to occur, not based on when the benefit of the spending will be recorded.

def•i•ni•tion

Sometimes called fixed assets, an **asset** is an accounting term used for items that are the result of a one-time transaction that provides a benefit for an extended period of time, normally the lifetime of the asset. For example, you may buy a company truck once, but the company benefits from it for as long as the truck remains in service.

Depreciation describes the spreading of the cost of an asset over multiple years. In our case, you may spend $10,000 on your trade show display but use it at multiple shows over two years, after which you have to buy a new one. Rather than recording a huge expense the day the display is bought, the cost of it is depreciated across two years.

Payment for Budget Items

There are a variety of show types and sizes, resulting in significant cost differences. The most effective system for show budgeting is to start by having a management-approved annual trade show budget to work with.

After you have this annual budget, you can then allocate the appropriate budget for each show at which you plan to exhibit. To speed the planning process further, use the defined system you discussed with your accounting department to pay for show-related costs. If a signed purchase order is part of your payment process and that process is slow in your organization, make sure to factor in this extra time so that you won't miss payment deadlines and discounts associated with those deadlines.

Show Smarts

If cash flow is an important consideration, ask the accounting department if you should consider paying for as many items as possible by credit card and ask which credit card should be used if you haven't already been supplied with one. Depending on the credit card used, this can add up to 50 days to the time you have to actually pay your expenses without incurring any interest charges.

Tracking Actual Costs

Tracking final costs in the budget spreadsheet is critical for conducting a thorough exhibit strategy analysis, which is conducted postshow. (You'll learn more about this in Chapter 20.) The total show costs are used to evaluate actual costs versus budget, ROI, cost per lead, and many other areas of analysis determined to be of relevance to your business.

One area of the evaluation reviews the actual show costs against estimated costs to decide where necessary or possible budget reductions can be made for future shows. ROI and cost per lead, compared against the final costs, are also part of the postshow evaluation. This will help determine whether the show provided enough sales to justify exhibiting at that show again.

The Least You Need to Know

- ◆ You need to develop a budget and track expenses if you want to be able to measure your ROI.

- ◆ There are 11 key areas to budget for, with a wide variety of expenses to estimate and track within each of these areas.

- ◆ Big-ticket items such as your booth display must be capitalized over multiple shows to accurately determine your true cost and return on a trade show.

- ◆ You may have to create a cash-flow budget in addition to your show's budget to see when you have to pay for each item and when your company will have to spend what funds on the trade show activities.

- ◆ If cash flow is tight for your company, pay by credit card for as many things as possible. This gives the accounting department extra interest-free time to pay for items.

- ◆ Tracking actual costs is essential to determine meaningful and accurate returns and to improve the budgeting process in the future.

Part 2

Planning: Space and Booth

Once you decide to exhibit, the real work begins. The first hurdle is understanding this complex thing called the "Exhibitor Guide." While this collection of rules and regulations is dry to read, it provides you with a wealth of information that you'll need to successfully plan the show.

The information from the guide combined with a good understanding of who you want to reach will help you design and create an effective booth. And because that display won't do you much good unless you occupy it with well-trained booth staffers, we'll also spend some time discussing how to select and train your trade show team.

4

The Devil Is in the Details

In This Chapter

- ◆ Components of the exhibitor kit
- ◆ Meeting various show deadlines
- ◆ Show rules and regulations to follow
- ◆ Show services often available
- ◆ Organizing your show paperwork

Now that you have selected and registered for a show, you will receive the exhibitor kit. This kit usually contains a huge amount of information, as well as all the forms you have to complete.

A couple of years ago, this kit would have been mailed to you in a large binder, jam-packed with all the show and convention facility forms. Few show producers follow that method anymore; the kits were costly to prepare and mail to each exhibitor. Most shows have moved to a more cost-efficient, web-based system. Most often you are provided with a link to the show's website, or the *show services company*, along with a username and password for secure access to the exhibitor kit. From here, you may choose to download all the paperwork from the site, create your own binder, and fax in the paperwork to the show. Another option some shows are beginning to provide is the ability to access all show details and fill in all order forms online.

It is tempting to skip over parts of the exhibitor kit that may seem less important. However, in this chapter, you learn there are many important details included in the kit that require your attention.

Exhibitor Kit Details

A good exhibitor kit contains everything relevant to exhibiting at that show. It covers details such as available services, show hours, setup and breakdown hours, insurance requirements, and rules and regulations.

Most exhibitor kits are similar. However, they are not identical. Areas that may differ include rules and regulations, union guidelines per city, and convention facility requirements. Treat the exhibitor kit like you would treat a contract for buying a house—read it from beginning to end, even if it feels painful!

def•i•ni•tion

A **show services company** is contracted by the show's producer to support her in creating the show, including theme, layout, signage, exhibitor kit components, etc. The show services company provides exhibitors with all information related to the show. Show services are ordered directly through that company, and it also provides show support both before and at the show.

Show Hours

As the name suggests, there are defined show hours. These can range greatly from a few hours on a single day for a table top show to more than a week with 10 show hours per day for a big international show. The show hour information also informs you when your booth staff is allowed on the floor before and after the actual show hours to set up for the day and shut down the booth at the close of the show.

Show Contacts

The exhibitor kit provides you with a list of contacts who are available to help you with the various areas of the show.

Depending on the show, contacts are listed either individually with their respective responsibilities or by department. Contact descriptions are also identified in a variety of ways.

These are the typical show contacts provided:

Exhibitor sales	Show manager
Registration	Show services
Exhibitor directory listing	Audio visual
Public relations	Catering
Advertising	Cleaning
Sponsorship	Electrical

Rules and Regulations

Rules and regulations vary greatly between each show and convention center, and they are usually very long and often printed in small print. Like most things in fine print, the rules and regulations contain the details that may result in unpleasant surprises if you don't read them thoroughly. These might include restrictions on height, audio, balloons, and food.

Don't Do It!

Let's say you plan to offer attendees water bottles that you purchased from an outside vendor. However, the rules written in small print state that water bottles can only be purchased from the show's caterer. Soon after the show opens, you will be told to cease handing them out; your only other option will be to repurchase them from the show's catering provider. This could be an expensive lesson to learn the hard way. Be sure to read the fine print carefully.

Union Guidelines

Union guidelines vary greatly by location. The word "guideline" suggests a degree of flexibility here that does not really exist. They are rules more than they are guidelines, and they are strictly enforced, so make sure you know what they are. If you are a small exhibitor bringing a pop-up display that you set up by yourself, you probably won't have much to worry about. If setting up your booth involves tools or even a ladder to put something on top of your display, it's time to pay attention to this section of the exhibitor kit very carefully.

Show-Specific Deadlines

Not surprisingly, there are a variety of deadlines associated with exhibiting at any show. There are some that are absolute deadlines that you must not miss in order to receive a certain benefit. For example, there will be a specific cutoff time by which you have to provide your company description to be listed in the show guide or on the show's website.

A benefit like this helps attendees intentionally find your company's booth rather than just run into it while walking down the aisles. Many decision makers create a schedule of booths to visit prior to the show when comparing products and companies; they don't aimlessly walk the show floor. If you miss this deadline, you miss potential opportunities.

Certificate of Insurance

Proof of insurance typically needs to be provided to the show by a certain deadline. The average requirements are a *certificate of liability insurance* carrying workers' compensation as required by individual state law; commercial general liability to include products and operations, independent contractors, and personal injury; and blanket contractual liability insurance of a defined amount (for example, $100,000 per occurrence, $500,000 aggregate). Additionally, the show's producer and the convention center need to be named as additional insured parties.

def•i•ni•tion

A **certificate of liability insurance** is evidence of the financial capability of a company to compensate for damage or loss incurred by its actions.

Exhibitor kits vary. Some have detailed insurance sections with examples; others mention requirements in the fine print of the rules and regulations. Always look for insurance requirements since noncompliance will typically prevent you from exhibiting.

Booth Staff Registration

Many shows are very accommodating and set no real limits when it comes to the number of exhibitor badges provided. Others provide only a fixed number as part of your exhibit package, requiring additional exhibitor badges to be purchased.

Most of the time, booth staff registration is done online. However, some shows still require a faxed registration list. In most cases, you provide the full name and job title for each staff member who requires an exhibitor badge.

Discounts for Services Ordered

The exhibitor kit will spell out ordering deadlines for show services. There is typically a decent discount for services ordered by a certain date, after which you pay regular rates. The discounts may range from $20 to $50 for smaller items, but they can save you hundreds of dollars on bigger-ticket items. Consequently, most services ordered while at the show require an additional on-site fee.

Do yourself a favor and be sure to meet the discount deadlines. You will save a significant amount of budget dollars that can be applied elsewhere.

Essential Shipping Details

Each show has specific shipping information outlining dates, warehousing, destination, and many other useful items related to getting your booth to and from the show. Shows often provide shipping labels and have a recommended shipping company, normally referred to as the show carrier.

While using the show carrier may help with the loading dock procedures, you can use any freight company you like. (Chapter 15 provides
detailed coverage of the shipping process.) If you are exhibiting at a
show outside your home country, be aware of customs requirements,
which are rarely found in an exhibitor kit. (Chapter 21 covers international exhibiting in detail.)

Display Shipping Location

There are two main shipping destination options. One option is the
advance warehouse, which is used as a holding place for shipments
going to the actual convention center. Shipments here typically arrive
as early as one month before the show. Having the time to correct
possible shipping problems is the main benefit of shipping items early.
Doing so, however, incurs warehousing and additional handling fees.

The other option is to ship to the show site, which saves you a fair
amount of money but leaves you with very limited time to deal with
any shipping troubles. Also, be aware that there are rules affecting the
times a shipping company has to check-in to the show, and the show
will normally not accept shipments outside those check-in times.

Freight Check-In Procedures

The freight check-in procedures define the times and process to be followed when your freight company delivers directly to the show site. It
must first check in at the marshalling yard by a defined time, which is
found in the exhibitor kit. The marshalling yard is essentially a holding
area for the shipping company.

The in-bound shipment process starts by first weighing each truck
upon arrival to obtain the gross, or heavy, weight. (Be sure the carrier
has the certified weight certificate and bill of lading with him.) Then
each driver is assigned a pass number and is directed to the loading
dock to off-load the shipment as space becomes available. After the
driver off-loads the shipment, he must head back to the marshalling
yard with his copy of the completed receiving report, where the truck
is weighed again to obtain the light weight. This process is followed to
verify and determine the total weight of the shipment.

The following is a list of common freight check-in procedure definitions:

♦ A **bill of lading** is a commercial shipping document that establishes a contract between the exhibitor and the freight company. It
also serves as a receipt. This document includes shipping charges,
descriptions of pickup and drop-off locations, freight check-in
deadlines at the show, the number of items transported, and a
description of the packaging and weight of the shipment.

♦ At pickup from the original location, the freight carrier will place
a **PRO number** on the paperwork. This PRO number is created
through a progressive numbering system and is used to identify
and track the shipment. Each piece that is shipped is tagged with
the PRO number. The carrier keeps a copy, and you get a copy of
the paperwork.

♦ **Gross weight** or **heavy weight** refers to the weight of the freight
truck including the shipment. This is obtained at check-in at the
marshalling yard.

♦ **Light weight** is the weight of the freight truck excluding the
weight of the shipment after off-loading it at the loading dock.
This is obtained at checkout from the marshalling yard.

♦ The **loading dock** is the area of the convention facility where
freight is received and off-loaded before it is delivered to the
exhibitor's booth.

♦ The **marshalling yard** is a holding location or lot, designated by
show services, where freight carriers report before and after deliveries are off-loaded at the loading dock. Trucks are weighed upon
arrival and before leaving to obtain shipment weight. The area
also functions as a trailer staging area throughout the duration of
a trade show.

♦ The **receiving report** is written notification that the shipment has
been off-loaded and is completed at the loading dock. This report
documents that the shipment was received and accepted by show
services. The shipment off-loaded at the dock is delivered to your
booth by show services.

Move-In and Move-Out Dates

Move-in and move-out dates typically vary by the size of the booth space ordered. Larger exhibits are given more time to be assembled, while smaller booths are often restricted to setting up the day before the event. In some cases, veteran exhibitors set up these booths the morning of the first show day. Newer exhibitors should plan on setting up as early as they are allowed.

Show Hotels

Bigger shows make special arrangements with at least one nearby hotel to offer discounted rates to exhibitors and attendees. These show hotels also frequently host networking or presentation events sponsored by the show itself or by larger exhibitors. If the hotel is not right by the convention center, shuttle bus service is provided in most cases.

Because show hotels host the majority of attendees, it is not uncommon for the breakfast buffet or the hotel lobby to turn into ad-hoc meeting and networking locations. On occasion, this enables you to make contact with individuals who are otherwise hard to reach on the show floor.

Show Colors Selected for Pipe and Drape

Each show selects colors for its standard pipe, drape, and carpet. Whether it is due to the twisted taste of show producers or the cost and availability of certain colors, these selections are sometimes hideous at best.

Check what colors are provided and, if necessary, consider spending the extra money to get the colors that match your display and corporate image. Renting black draping for the back and side rails works well for just about every booth and makes your display and *messaging* stand out. Also, renting black carpeting with this combination helps give a polished look to the booth. In any case, ordering drapes and skirting in colors matching or complementing the colors of your exhibit will make a big difference. The same applies to any table skirting you may order.

def•i•ni•tion

> The term **messaging** gets applied to a wide variety of marketing materials, but it is basically just text, communicating key points or action items you want the reader to do.
>
> As it relates to messaging for your display pieces, it is written to persuade or direct prospects to visit your booth or to suggest questions to ask, essentially the key points you want to plant in their minds.

Booth Enhancement Items to Rent

Any show but table top expos will offer a variety of rental options to complement your display and exhibiting material. The most important ones follow here.

Variety of Furniture

Furniture rentals range from basic tables with skirting to complete couch and coffee table sets fit to grace a luxury hotel's presidential suite. Most shows offer furniture sets on two package levels. A standard selection consists of reasonable furniture items. Additionally, there are higher-class items available that tend to be more modern in design, such as what you'd find in the show room of a luxury-brand car dealership.

Carpet and Padding

Carpets usually come in standard and deluxe and in more colors than a rainbow has to offer; however, as already mentioned, consider black as the color of choice. The main difference between standard and deluxe carpeting is the thickness of the carpet, providing a somewhat more prestigious feel if you choose the higher-priced option. For most businesses, the standard carpet option will be just fine.

More important than carpeting is padding since it greatly enhances

Don't Do It!

One layer of padding is great, but don't go overboard. Renting two or more layers gives your booth floor the feel of a sandy beach, and your booth staffers' feet and legs will feel as tired as they would after a day of walking in sand.

the comfort of your floor. While attendees may not notice, it often makes the difference between booth staffers who are lively and those who are hurting on the second day. If at all possible, find a way to make padding part of your budget.

Floral and Plant Rental

A simple fern can brighten up your booth and can be a wonderful help in hiding wires or other unsightly things that take away from your booth image. A wide variety of plants, from floor plants to trees to floral arrangements, are available. Just be careful to pick items that complement your booth, not items that clash with the image you want to portray at that show.

Ask the rental company for suggestions if you don't know much about flowers and plants. You can probably find samples of the options on its website, or you can do a Google image search and find pictures of the various plant, tree, and floral options available.

Labor Services

A number of labor services are available, ranging from help with setting up your display to electrical services to providing lifts to hang up ceiling signage. Keep in mind that labor services typically are billed in one-hour increments, even if the actual task is done in five minutes.

Hours are billed in straight time, overtime, and double-time rates. Union guidelines are often applicable and are covered in the Union Guidelines section of the exhibitor kit. If you are allowed by the show to select and bring in your own contractors, you have to submit an exhibitor-appointed contractor approval request form to the show producers.

Material Handling

The basic description of material handling is the movement of your show materials shipped to the convention facility. This includes a variety of services. One example is the delivery of your show materials to your booth at show opening and from your booth to the dock at show closing.

To help you fill in the material handling form from the exhibitor kit, remember these essentials. Charges are entirely based on the weight of your shipment, with the weight always being rounded up to the next 100 pounds. One "cwt" is the equivalent of 100 pounds. You are better off sending your shipment all at one time because there is a 200-pound minimum charge to factor in, even if the shipment weighs much less.

Booth Cleaning

Booth cleaning services are usually available at trade shows, although they are optional. They include vacuum cleaning the booth floor overnight as well as garbage removal. Having a clean and tidy booth is an important part of the impression you make on attendees, so it is certainly a service worth considering.

Budget Savers

If you choose not to order booth cleaning services, a great money-saving tip is to bring several larger-size sticky lint rollers to clean up the carpet before the show opens. This obviously takes more work, and you need to get down on your hands and knees to do this task. It comes down to whether your company is more interested in saving time or money. Another option is a cordless sweeper; however, consider the weight when purchasing and determine what the shipping and material handling costs will be if you require those services.

Storage: Entire Show or Accessible Anytime

If you don't have enough storage space within your display or under a skirted table, you have to rent storage space. Use the lower-priced show storage facility to store shipping containers or similar items that you will not need to reuse until packing up and shipping back your booth.

Items for which you have no space in the booth but that you need to access during the show, such as promotional items, need to be kept in the accessible storage area. Keep in mind that anytime you access the items, you have to pay material handling charges. The items are brought directly to your booth by show services, which can create a sizeable bill if you need to access the area often.

Budget Savers

If you are in a convention facility that allows exhibitors to carry in items, consider saving storage costs altogether by storing items in your hotel room.

If there are many items to store, have several booth staffers keep supplies in their rooms as well. Keep a master list of who has each item, note when you access each item, and keep an inventory list. Have a sturdy, foldable cart with you for transporting the materials to the convention facility.

Technical Services

A host of technical services are available to exhibitors, such as audio-visual equipment rentals, lead capture devices, and Internet services. You often find phone service as an option as well, though in today's cell phone world this is really obsolete unless you need one for a telephone-line-based credit card processing machine.

Since you may already own some of these pieces of equipment, such as monitors and projectors, you may be tempted to use your own items. But consider the loss of use of those items in the office while you are at the show and the possibility of damaging them in transit. You also need to factor in the weight and material handling prices when deciding whether to ship your own items or rent equipment at the show. In addition, unless one of your booth staffers is technically savvy, you may not have someone available to troubleshoot problems with equipment. When renting, you save shipping and material handling charges and have on-site technicians responsible for ensuring that your rental works properly.

Audio-Visual Equipment and Services

You can always bring your own audio-visual equipment. The main benefit of renting is that there is an immediate replacement available if needed. Trying to get a replacement for something as simple as a bulb for your projector might be quite an undertaking, whereas a rental device comes with on-site help that can replace items in the time it takes you to find a phone number for a vendor that will have your bulb.

Typical audio-visual items available for rental include projectors, computers, laptops, flat-screen monitors, high-speed Internet, and printers. Show services will outsource to a reputable audio-visual company, which you will pay directly. Follow instructions on the audio-visual order form to place your order directly with them. On site, there will be a help desk available to order extra equipment or dispatch help over to your booth.

Lead Capture Machine Rental

Almost every show offers lead capture devices for rent. These devices are good for capturing information for a marketing database. Most often you can't ask questions about prospects' needs, such as purchasing timeframe, product interest, and decision-making level, which are crucial to the sales follow-up process. The devices vary greatly in size and complexity. Some are simply bar code readers with a simple printer or data storage device, and some are sophisticated PDA's with card scanners that access a central storage through WiFi.

A lead system that is truly useful to your sales organization needs the ability to qualify prospects by asking questions. If questions can't be programmed into the lead capture device, you are much better off buying your own lead capturing equipment or even resorting to a paper questionnaire that the prospects or your booth staff fill in. If you decide to stick with the lead capture device provided in the exhibitor kit, you need to order it directly from the contracted vendor.

Internet Services

Internet services are increasingly important, even to exhibitors who don't depend on showing Internet-based products or services. Having an Internet connection at your booth may allow you to connect a custom lead capturing system to your customer relationship management (CRM) software back in the office, or it may allow demonstrations of navigating your company website for specific information.

While show floors are increasingly covered by free WiFi Internet, having your own Internet connection might still be worthwhile if you need the reliability of a wired connection or if you might be using Internet features that are blocked on the free WiFi service. Internet service is typically ordered through the audio-visual company listed in the exhibitor kit.

Miscellaneous Items

To help increase both your ROI and that of the show, all shows offer some additional services beyond the ones in the categories already discussed. The usefulness of these is very specific to your individual situation and should be considered accordingly.

Food and Beverage

Food and beverages are often a good way to get attendees into your booth space. However, if you are trying to attract only a small, specific segment of the attendees, food and beverages are not the best choice. Attendees get hungry and thirsty whether they are in your target group or not. Should you elect to provide food and beverages at your booth, make sure to check the rules and regulations to see if you are required to purchase those items from show services or if you are allowed to bring in your own catering contractors.

Booth Photography

Booth photography can be a good option if you are looking for professional photos for follow-up coverage of your booth. Reasons for booth photography might include a trade show report, cataloging booth designs over the years, publishing your booth on your corporate website so that attendees can easily find you, or creating specific marketing materials where having a picture of your booth is helpful.

Security Items

While most shows will provide some sort of overnight security, leaving high-value items in the booth overnight is seldom a good idea. So if you don't want to drag those items back and forth from the hotel, renting a padlocked cage or a safe at the show might be a good option.

Display Options and Graphic Design Services

Many shows now offer complete booth rentals, which include every-thing from signage to furniture. Sometimes using these services makes sense. For example, if you are exhibiting at more than one event at the same time, buying a second exhibit does not make financial sense.

Renting a complete booth might also be a good option for companies that want to test the waters of trade show exhibiting, preferring to try it without the expenditure of owning your own display. Also, if your display gets lost or severely damaged during transport, those services might be your only option to save your show.

Ordering Services

As previously discussed, some shows offer online ordering of services, while others only have the exhibitor kit forms for you to complete for each service. When ordering services with the paper forms, fill in con-tact information, rental items or services you are ordering, and then add up the total costs on each page. A separate form, commonly referred to as the method of payment form, accompanies your order. On this form, fill in all contact information, method of payment, and add up the totals for each service you are ordering. Then write the grand total.

Special services such as floral, Internet, audio-visual, electricity, booth photography, and so on are provided by different vendors. You need to fill in those forms separately and follow their ordering instructions. All these forms come with the exhibitor kit:

◆ **Review exhibit package purchased and inclusions:** The exhibit package you selected may already include some of the items that are also offered as options. So before ordering any services or rentals, make sure they are not already part of your package.

◆ **Saving time or money:** Most optional items boil down to saving either money or time. Using show services is very convenient, but this convenience comes at a price. A big plus of show-provided options is that they eliminate some of the risk associated with using third-party vendors. Items rented from the show never get lost in shipping.

♦ **Determining what to order:** The decision as to what to order largely depends on your available resources. While you should always be cost conscious and try to save money when reasonably possible, you should have a specific show budget (as determined in the previous chapter). Make a list of your ideal options and tally them up to see if they fit within your budget. If they do, think twice about each option and if it provides the value it costs. If your dream list does not fit within your budget, identify the items you can do without and cut things as much as needed.

 In Chapter 4 of the CD, you will find a master planning checklist, a planning meeting checklist, binder tabs for your planning binder as well as where to place paperwork from the exhibitor kit, a suggested supplies spreadsheet, and a supplies spreadsheet already filled in.

Organizing and Managing Information

Keeping track of all the orders you are placing, along with the many other items related to a trade show, will require a great deal of organization. Having both paper and electronic copies of information is crucial to eliminating loss of information. One system for organizing show-related information is to have a master show binder with paper copies of all items as well as an electronic copy of all paperwork located in folders on your computer. Also have a master show planning checklist, preferably on your computer, and add it to the binder when it gets updated.

The Least You Need to Know

♦ Read the exhibitor kit carefully, including rules and regulations.

♦ Know what's included in your exhibitor package before considering optional services.

♦ Make sure any optional services you may want fit into your overall budget before ordering them.

♦ Follow the show planning checklist to make sure you don't forget important items.

Chapter 5

Creating an Effective Booth

In This Chapter

- ◆ Learn the three main purposes of your booth and how your show objectives affect the design

- ◆ Identify the different booth configurations and how to make the best use of them

- ◆ Learn how to create an effective booth layout

- ◆ Keep your booth safe by following the necessary requirements

- ◆ Use your collateral location as a means to get attendees to enter your booth

Assuming you have been to a trade show, you know that there are many creative and unique booth designs. Your objective is to come up with a design that not only stands out and attracts attention, but also meets the goals and objectives of your exhibiting plan. Based on criteria you have determined, creating a functional and appealing layout requires careful thought and strategic planning, well in advance of the show. In the design of your booth space, limits are largely set by your imagination. This chapter shows you how to design an engaging booth space, one that draws attendees into the environment you have created in order for them to learn more about your products.

Regardless of the size of a booth, you can learn how to control *traffic flow* and entice attendees into your booth by placing items that they want in areas inside the booth. Then you are able to approach the attendees for a conversation. This includes an area for capturing leads, providing space for meetings, and demonstrating products.

Purposes of the Booth

There are three primary booth functions. Depending on your show goals, the order of importance may vary but the same three functions are always present. Your booth needs to be able to cope with traffic, provide space to interact with attendees, and attract visitors to the booth.

def•i•ni•tion

Traffic flow is the direction or path you create in your booth layout that is used to direct attendees' movement through your exhibit space. You can also create barriers to limit traffic flow so that qualified audiences feel invited to visit your booth and comfortable that they will receive more individualized attention to discuss their product needs.

Each booth size brings its own list of challenges. A big booth has plenty of space to work with, but you still have to find a design that accommodates all traffic and makes it easy for attendees to locate the right demonstration station or product-specific experts. The problems you face in the design of a large booth are quite different from the challenges faced in the design of a small booth, where you have to be rather creative to maximize space utilization without sacrificing an appealing design. Anyone who has seen a Pontiac Aztec understands what I mean by sacrificing look for functionality!

Prospect Traffic

A key design consideration is the amount of traffic you expect and how you wish to handle it. For example, your primary goal may be to promote the branding of your company and generate interest in your products. In this case, your booth layout should be designed to cope with large numbers of people and provide presentations simultaneously to many attendees. You should also provide enticing incentives or promotional items to draw attendees into your booth.

On the other hand, you may be looking to attract relatively small numbers of highly qualified attendees who will then be given more personalized attention. For this purpose, you want to limit the amount of random traffic coming in the booth. This booth design should be less open and focus more on placing road blocks that reduce the number of unqualified prospects entering your interaction space.

Prospect Interaction

A prospect interaction area can fit into any booth that is bigger than a table top. The size and implementation of this area depends on your booth size. For example, a small, high-top, round table and a couple of bar stools fit into any booth, even a 10'×10', and can provide prospects and sales staff with a dedicated space to spend quality time discussing the prospect's needs and your solutions.

If you have a larger booth, you can go with couches, lounge chairs, and coffee tables. Sometimes a bar area with booth staffers serving drinks can be an attractive option. Be creative with the options and budget available to you and design areas that allow good interaction with your prospects.

 Don't Do It!

You want to create an area where your booth staffers can interact with prospects. Be careful not to create a general "rest area" where attendees try to hang out to rest their feet.

Create an Inviting Environment

Creating an inviting environment is often a balancing act between staying within the corporate look and feel and creating a unique style and experience designed with the tastes of your target prospects in mind. To be successful at that, use components of the corporate image or even a theme that attracts your key prospects. Use a layout that creates attention and invites prospects to enter the booth, providing booth staffers the opportunity to engage them and learn more about the attendees' needs.

To pick the best possible option, create multiple booth layouts that incorporate different design aspects and themes and then evaluate which one best supports your objectives.

Booth Configurations

Any show that is not a table top expo offers a variety of booth configuration options. There are also various restrictions and limitations. For example, there are always height restrictions designed to equalize the playing field, giving each booth an opportunity to be seen. Height restrictions can be quite different from show to show. In the case of international shows, though, they are often more liberal and allow two-story booths, with meeting space located on a second floor.

Not only does each show offer different configuration options, but the layout for booth aisles also varies. Traditionally, shows have offered rows and rows of inline booths. However, more shows have moved increasingly toward 20'×20' cubes, often split into four 10'×10' booths, giving each booth a corner location. These layouts appeal to exhibitors because they provide attendees with more access areas for entering the booth and more options for exhibitors to have signage seen.

In-Line Booths

As the name suggests, these booths are in a line and represent the most common layout. The show features lines of 10'×10' booths with the occasional 10'×20' booth mixed in. If you exhibit at such a show, registering early pays off big time since getting a corner location is highly desirable and booth space is almost always assigned on a first-come, first-served basis. It's always worth checking with the show, but typical height restrictions for a 10'×10' booth are between 8 and 10 feet. The display type used most often for a booth that size is a pop-up display.

Budget Savers

While pop-up displays are the most common displays for in-line booths, similar effects can be achieved through the clever use of banners at a much lower cost. You can use the back wall of your booth to hang up a large banner at a fraction of the cost of a full pop-up display.

Island Booths

Although I once saw a really cool booth that had a moat, complete with water and little bridges, the term *island configuration* is not really as interesting as that example makes it sound. Normally, it has nothing do with water. It simply means that the booth has an aisle on every side and does not border directly with any other booth.

Height restrictions tend to be in the neighborhood of 16 feet, and it is often possible to have a two-story booth. The booth size is typically 400 square feet or larger. A booth this size normally requires a custom-built display, which, combined with the cost of the show floor space, requires a sizable budget.

Peninsula Booths

As with regular real estate, a peninsula is not quite as desirable as an island, but it is the next best thing. A peninsula has aisles on three sides, and its forth side borders either the show hall wall or another booth.

While the majority of peninsula booths are 20'×20' or larger, you can find lower-cost peninsula booths at the end of some in-line configurations where an exhibitor has two 10'×10' corner booths combined to create a 10'×20' peninsula.

Corner Booths

A corner booth has aisles on two sides, with the other two sides facing either a wall or other booths. In most cases, the booths are divided up with drapes clearly marking the assigned space.

Partner Pods or Kiosks

Sometimes associations or large companies rent a significant amount of exhibit space and provide small demonstration stations, often called "pods" or "kiosks," for their partners or members. Although these pods and kiosks are not booth types, they are possible trade show options.

These options are often a cheap way for an exhibitor to participate in a trade show, but they come with restrictions. In the case of a partner pavilion, you may only show products that complement the sponsor's products and services; in the case of a shared booth, you have to be part of that association to participate. Similar to a table top expo, your ability to make changes to your demonstration station or pod is limited. Typically, you are restricted from making your booth stand out from the others in any way. The look of your booth must be uniform to the look of the other "stations."

Typical Booth Sizes Offered

The majority of booths at any trade show are 10'×10' or 10'×20' because those sizes are the most affordable when it comes to booth space pricing and display costs. For example, those booth sizes accommodate pop-up displays, which can normally be set up by the exhibitor, avoiding various labor and handling fees.

Create an Inviting Booth Layout

Creating an inviting booth layout starts with a draft. On occasion that will be a drawing on a napkin, but most of the time computer-aided design works out better. Working with a display vendor is helpful because those companies assist you in designing and developing various possible layouts.

Designing a booth is not unlike designing a building. Start by drawing up several general layout options based on the primary items you need to have in your booth. Then consider adding extras such as food stations or smaller items such as plants, special lightning, or individual banner stands.

Show Smarts

If you have a large display, you need to complete the show's booth layout form along with any orders for optional items such as carpeting, padding, electric wiring, signs, and so on. The form typically requires a drawing illustrating where those optional items are to be placed.

Engaging Items for Attendees

You only have a couple seconds to grab the attention of someone strolling down the aisles. It's important to make those seconds count toward drawing your target prospects into your booth. Messaging, discussed in Chapter 8, is a key component to achieving this goal. Beyond messaging, appeal to all the senses. Use sights, sounds, and, if appropriate, smell to get the attendees' attention and to get them to step into your booth.

Primary Display and Other Signage

The content of the display and signage is usually more important than any other design or material used. With that said, the design and materials need to support the image of your company as well as the messages you are communicating. There are wide varieties of display types and components to choose from, such as simple pop-up displays, fabric displays, modular displays, and custom-built displays. Creatively designed displays and signage generate interest and attention in your exhibit space.

Presentation

Presentation options come in many flavors, from a homegrown, basic, scrolling Microsoft PowerPoint presentation to professionally produced videos and live presenters. In most cases, it is a very good idea to have some type of presentation going on at your booth for attendees to stop and watch. Anything that moves and makes noise catches people's attention and can help draw in visitors. It should be entertaining and informational, giving attendees something to watch while they wait to speak to a specific member of your booth team or simply to obtain information.

If you are doing live presentations, make sure to post a schedule so that attendees know when to be back at your booth. It's also a good idea to offer promotional items to attendees who watch an entire presentation and then complete a lead form.

Lighting

Lighting is an interesting tool for creating attention or atmosphere. In the most basic form, it is used to highlight something, typically a sign. Colored lighting can be used quite effectively to create a mood such as excitement/energy, peace, or friendliness. Multicolored lighting, especially the type that continuously changes, draws the eye toward the booth, creating interest and attracting attention. But be careful not to overdo it—you don't want your booth to look like a dance club.

Food and Beverages

Booths that offer food or beverages are popular, and not only because the food and beverage options at convention centers tend to make airport snacks look cheap. People like free food, period.

Having food and drinks is a sure way to attract a crowd. The downside is you may not want that crowd since it typically consists of hungry, thirsty people rather than qualified prospects for your products and services. Also, offering food and beverages can be very costly, especially if the show requires you to buy them from show services.

Show Smarts

Before adding food and beverage options to your exhibit plan, always check the show's rules and regulations to find out whether those items are allowed and if they have to be bought from a specific supplier.

Purchasing from a specific supplier, typically the convention facility's food services provider, can be quite costly. Knowing this information will also allow you to determine costs for your budget and whether this cost even fits into your available budget.

Flowers or Plants

Floral pieces or plants are a good way to add a finishing touch to a booth. They can make the difference between a plain booth and a booth with atmosphere. Flowers and plants are also a great way to hide things you don't want to be seen, such as cabling or small blemishes on your display.

Prospect Interaction Areas

As previously mentioned, prospect interaction areas can significantly impact your success at the show, depending on who you sell to and how you sell. In many cases, having a separate interaction space away from other attendees or booth components will suffice. However, having a seating area to discuss products and customer needs can make the difference between a collected lead and an actual sale.

Enabling attendees to get off their feet for a few minutes will increase their willingness to spend more time with your booth staffers. Another important reason for providing a comfortable environment is to help prospects see your attention to detail and customer service, which can increase their comfort level with your products and company.

Furniture

Odds are, at some point in your life you've been shopping for furniture, so I don't have to tell you that there are virtually limitless options. If you have a custom display, you may have specifically designed seating areas and custom furniture already. If not, you can rent furniture from the show and independent vendors as well. I've also seen exhibitors stop by a local Ikea store before a show and then just give the items to local show workers since shipping the items would have been more expensive than buying them again. You can also donate them to local charities, which will usually be willing to pick the items up; you may even end up with a tax-deductible donation.

Rental options start with basic furniture and then move up toward the trendiest items found in the hippest club around. It's a matter of budget, your corporate image, and the prospect types you are looking to reach.

Lead Capture Location

Even a small booth needs some type of dedicated area for lead capturing, away from the main demonstration or discussion areas. The bigger your booth, the more lead collection stations or areas you need.

Lead collection stations should not be located directly at the booth's entrance, where attendees may feel they will get pounced upon for their contact information once they get close to your booth.

Show Smarts

Even if you have an electronic lead capturing system, have paper forms available in case your booth becomes too busy for the device to handle the traffic or in case you experience technical difficulty with your electronic system.

Informational Collateral

You need to have *collateral* available for your prospects to complement presentations or personal discussions that take place. Collateral should be placed centrally in the booth, requiring attendees to actually enter the booth to get it. Having it on the sides of your booth results in visitors walking by and simply grabbing the piece of information they want. This is detrimental to your efforts at engaging attendees and qualifying them.

def•i•ni•tion

> **Collateral** is the combination of media used to support the sales of goods or services. They are considered sales tools to simplify and shorten the sales cycles. Typical examples include brochures and data sheets, but also include sales scripts, videos, web content, etc.

Have a booth staffer work near the collateral station and engage attendees that have not been attended to yet. The staffer can make an educated guess as to what the visitor is looking for based on the collateral the attendee picks up, which makes it even easier to start a conversation.

Electrical Layout and Requirements

While there are many requirements worth paying attention to, clearly the most important one is the electrical requirements. If you have any uncertainties whatsoever, check with the show or consult with a professional, licensed electrician.

Carelessness, improper use, and faulty wiring make electrical issues the single biggest reason for fires at trade shows. While a fire at your booth is sure to attract attention, the attention will be short-lived, will not result in qualified leads, and will leave a bad impression of your company on attendees.

All convention facilities reserve the right to inspect your exhibit, without notice, as well as its wiring and electrical setup to verify compliance with requirements. Any deviation has to be corrected by the show electrician at your expense. Noncompliance usually results in electricity being disconnected altogether.

Show Smarts

If you are exhibiting for the first time and don't have much experience with the actual size of a booth, find yourself some space in the office and tape off the size of your booth on the floor. This helps you get a much better feel for the amount of space you have to work with.

If possible, leave the taped area intact for a while so that you can use it as a reference when you look at purchasing or renting items. Simply tape those dimensions off to get a good feel for how they fit into your booth space.

The Least You Need to Know

♦ Define your booth layout based on the primary goals of your show, such as getting qualified leads or creating awareness of a product or service.

♦ Prospect interaction areas allow you to confer with prospects without interrupting the other show activities.

♦ Use presentations to inform visitors and attract them to your booth.

♦ Pay attention to important requirements such as electricity to avoid problems or injuries.

♦ Use space-maximizing items such as individual banner stands to get the most out of your available space.

Chapter 6

Selecting the Display Type and Accessories

In This Chapter

◆ Figure out what display options you have and what you can afford

◆ Both purchasing and renting have their advantages; find out which option is right for you

◆ Pick a display type considering the type of flexibility you may need to grow or modify your exhibit

◆ Learn how to use accessories to complement your booth

◆ Use lighting to emphasize your booth or certain aspects of it

Display options are available for every budget and imagination, and new and creative products enter the market every day. So finding one won't be the problem, but making the right decision is a different story. This chapter helps you understand what you need to know to choose the display that will fit your budget and exhibiting objectives. Keep in mind that, when you talk to display vendors, their interest is to sell you whatever benefits them most.

The knowledge from this chapter will put you in a better position to make informed decisions and to guide conversations with display vendors in the direction you need them to go. With all that said, there are many really good vendors out there that are perfectly willing and capable to find the product most suited for your company's exhibit program.

Display Selection Guidelines

Before you go booth shopping, you need to know the likely booth size for your exhibit. Many designs are suitable for more than one size by using or leaving out certain components. You also need to keep in mind your exhibiting objectives and any "vision" you already have for how it should look. If you have a bigger booth, think about what activities will occur in the booth, such as product demonstrations, product display, entertainment, theatre presentations, meeting areas, lead-collection terminals, and so on. The more you know about your booth's needs, the easier it is for you to explain to vendors what you are looking for, and the more likely you are to get what you want.

Display Items You Currently Have

Take a look at what you currently have to work with and list all of those items. Then decide whether those items are up-to-date, if they still represent your company's image, and if they coincide with what you have learned in this book. If the display is more than five years old, chances are good that it is out of style with current trends and the evolution of your company, and there probably won't be that much to salvage. At a minimum, you will need to upgrade the graphics or quite possibly purchase a newer type of display style.

Display Budget

If you don't already have an allotted budget for your display or at least a price range to guide you, figure out what you want and what you can spend before making any calls to display vendors. The sky is the limit for display pricing, so you don't want to waste time having display vendors design things that are outside your price range.

Purchase or Rent

Depending on your exhibiting needs, renting a display might be a worthwhile consideration. If you are overbooked and exhibiting at two shows at the same time or if it is your first trade show, then a rental may be the smarter choice for you. If it is your first trade show, renting enables you to look at the other displays while at the show and get a better feel for how they look on the show floor and how they work for products and companies in your industry. If you have exhibited before and are certain of the display type that best suits your needs, and if you expect to exhibit multiple times in a similar booth size, then you're better off purchasing the display.

Self Setup Displays for Small Booths

Self setup displays are a good choice for small booths. They usually come in their own wheeled shipping case, making them very portable. Graphics and accessories fit inside the casing, so you can often fit the entire exhibit into a car, check it in for a flight, or ship it at a reasonable rate. A well-made portable display should last you for quite a number of shows. You can simply make changes to the graphics but keep the rest intact.

As your company and messaging changes, so does your booth. The core components (such as the frame itself) stay the same, so you only have an incremental cost for any *look-and-feel* items you choose to change. An important aspect to consider, though, is that there can be significant differences in quality and craftsmanship. While all displays roughly look alike in brochures, they might look very different after a couple of shows. As a rule of thumb, you get what you pay for. It would not be a bad idea to ask for some reference customers before you buy to see how the displays are behaving.

def•i•ni•tion

Look and feel is a term used in marketing to describe the experience a customer or user has with a particular product or its main features. In this context, it describes the experience an attendee has with a booth and the elements that contribute to that.

Pop-Up Displays

Pop-up displays are made of an expandable, sort of telescopic or otherwise collapsible base frame that extends to create a back wall for your
booth. This back wall just pops up, hence the name. They are very
quick and easy to assemble and to dismantle and usually come in their
own container, which sometimes has wheels for easier transportation.
The back frame is covered with either printed panels or fabric. In the
case of fabric, Velcro® is used to attach graphics and signage and supports pretty much any shape and form. Pop-up displays are popular
because of their fairly low price. The downside to the pop-up display is
that it is hard to stand out with one. Sometimes a basic pop-up display
combined with a simple kiosk can create a more sophisticated look.

In Chapter 6 of the CD, you will find color display examples of
the images you see in this chapter, starting with a pop-up display.
The illustrations have been designed and provided by Expodepot.
com.

Pop-up display example.

(Sample image provided by Expodepot.com)

Panel Displays

As the name suggests, panel displays consist of thin, flat panels that use limited space when stacked on top of each other for shipping or storage. Panel systems are available in a wide range of models and styles and consist of either individual panels that are connected at the show or ones that are permanently connected and simply unfold. As with pop-up displays, if you use fabric with panels, then graphics can be attached using Velcro. While not quite as easy and quick to set up as pop-up displays, panel displays are usually stronger and can hold some weight such as presentation monitors, plants, or collateral holders.

 In Chapter 6 of the CD, you will find a panel display color image.

Panel display.

(Sample image provided by Expodepot.com)

Table Top Show Displays

Table top display options have come a long way over the years and now offer some interesting options that go well beyond a boring science-fair look. Display manufacturers finally noticed the need to provide better options for the large market of table top exhibitors who were painfully lacking modern-looking options. Most of the portable display options in this chapter have miniature counterparts for table top exhibiting. Panel displays often come as briefcases that fold open into a ready-to-go display. Pop-up displays come in assorted sizes and shapes suitable for table top exhibiting. Fabric/tension displays are flat or curved in different directions. You can also choose from backlit displays that cleverly convert from a table top display to a podium, making it multi-functional. Finally, there is the topper, which is ultramodern with many creative styles to choose from.

 In Chapter 6 of the CD, you will find a table top show display color image.

Table top show display example.

(Sample image provided by Expodepot.com)

Flexible Displays: Small or Large Booths

If you plan to exhibit in a variety of booth sizes, you need a flexible, scalable display that can be reconfigured as needed. Several display types are like an oversized LEGO® kit that you can use to reassemble your booth in various styles, sizes, and configurations.

Fabric/Tension Displays

Fabric/tension displays are a little like pop-up displays on steroids. They also provide a seamless graphic back wall, which gives you a couple of great options since they support shapes that a pop-up display will not. This gives fabric/tension displays a much more sophisticated and modern look. Because of their low cost but more modern look, I expect fabric/tension displays to replace pop-ups as the most popular display type. With various shapes available, it is easier to look different, and customization is fairly easy and affordable.

 In Chapter 6 of the CD, you will find a fabric/tension display color image.

Fabric/tension display example.

(Sample image provided by Expodepot.com)

Modular Displays

Modular displays are designed to be assembled in different configurations, making them ideal for exhibitors with frequently varying booth sizes. If well done, they look similar to a full custom display. Modular systems are composed of various modules (such as frames or panels) that can be connected to create the display in different combinations. They make great starter kits that can be enhanced over time as your company and exhibiting needs grow. Also, you can fairly easily replace individual parts that get lost or damaged. The downside is that these systems are heavier than portable displays, so shipping costs are higher, but they are still lighter than most custom displays.

In Chapter 6 of the CD, you will find a modular display color image.

Modular display example.

(Sample image provided by Expodepot.com)

Truss Displays

Truss displays are often used as specific components of a larger booth, but they are flexible and can also be used to build a complete display. We talked about Lego pieces earlier. Truss components are the smallest Lego pieces and provide the greatest amount of flexibility. They provide the building blocks for a limitless number of variations. Truss components are usually round, box-shape, triangular, or flat pieces designed for an easy assembly process that, unlike the real Lego, requires tools. Truss pieces are constructed of durable steel or composite material and are capable of supporting heavier items such as monitors, lights, or even collateral. Truss components are available in multiple colors and can be used to create artistic displays.

In Chapter 6 of the CD, you will find a truss display color image.

Sample Display Image courtesy of
www.ExpoDepot.com

Truss display example.

(Sample image provided by Expodepot.com)

Kiosks

Kiosks are great places to engage visitors or demo products. They usually have a place to mount a flat-panel monitor, which makes them ideal for showing presentations or showcasing computer software. They also have counter surfaces, providing space for notes, collecting leads, or a mouse and keyboard. Kiosks are not only functional, they give a booth a more sophisticated look. A low-cost panel or fabric background combined with a modern-looking kiosk makes a well-rounded impression. In general, kiosks are a great way to add dimension to your display.

In Chapter 6 of the CD, you will find a kiosk display color image.

Kiosk display example.

(Sample image provided by Expodepot.com)

Custom Designed and Built

Of course, there is nothing more individual than a designed display. Because the display is specific to your needs, it will certainly be unique. Unfortunately, custom-designed displays are also by far the most expensive option. These high-end displays are usually constructed of wood, metal, or composite material. It is possible to create pretty much anything you might want, from marble floors (which, of course, are expensive to ship) to multistory structures. Typically, custom displays are shipped in wooden crates that have to be moved with a forklift and shipped via freight line.

Note: A very knowledgeable resource available to answer your questions about custom exhibits is Ben Nazario from MC-2; he has been in the trade show industry for nearly two decades. You can reach Ben at bnazario@mc-2.com or on the website www.mc-2.com.

Budget-Conscious Display Options

There are many ways to keep your budget down but still present a professional image. Consider banners, pipe and drape sets, and used displays. The key to a budget-conscious booth is creativity. But keep in mind, even though you need to be budget conscious, you shouldn't sacrifice your brand or company image in the process. Select options that are inexpensive but not cheap looking. There is a big difference between the two.

Pipe and Drape Sets

Like anything else, pipe and drape systems come in various styles and sizes, ranging from modern styles to something King Louis X would have found appealing. Drapes should be made from durable, fire-resistant fabric designed specifically for trade shows and events. If you intend to purchase a set, make sure it is compliant with fire standards. Pipe and drape sets can be plain or printed, accommodating any style. They are easily transportable and fold into a suitcase or even a briefcase. Draping sets typically attach directly over the existing pipe and drape with simple clips.

 In Chapter 6 of the CD, you will find a pipe and drape set color image.

Banner Stands

Banner stands come in different sizes and can be the poor man's version of a pop-up background because they can hold a large, seamless graphic. Banner displays can be set up even faster than pop-up displays, and smaller versions are a great way to complement a display. Later in this book I will explain why I am a big fan of using banner stands, which come in many shapes and sizes to fit any need, to attract attention to a booth.

 In Chapter 6 of the CD, you will find a banner stand color image.

Pipe and drape display example.

(Sample image provided by Expodepot.com)

Banner stand display example.

(Sample image provided by Expodepot.com)

Used Displays

You can find used displays from a variety of sources such as vendors, ads in newspapers, and online. (There are almost always a few sellers on eBay®.) Most used displays are in very good shape. There are many reasons why companies decide to sell their exhibit properties. The main reason is that they are updating their look.

If you are considering buying a used display, ask the following questions to help your decision process:

◆ Is there any warranty left on the unit?

◆ How many times was the display used?

◆ How was the display packed and shipped?

◆ How many years have you owned the display?

◆ How was the display stored?

◆ Was it stored in a climate-controlled facility?

◆ Are there setup instructions included? Do you need labor to set up the booth, or can it be assembled by regular staff?

◆ Are all original parts of the display being sold, including any necessary tools to put the display together? Are there pieces missing? If yes, what are they?

◆ Can the item be returned if it does not meet the description?

You can, of course, add to this list, but this is a good way to start the conversation.

 Chapter 6 of the CD provides you with questions to ask when considering used displays.

Accessories

Accessories provide the finishing touches that support the activities and promotions in your booth. These items help you showcase a structured appearance.

Accessory possibilities are limitless, as are possible sources to find them. While some may be purchased from a traditional display vendor, others can be found at your local craft or furniture store. It depends on your market and the look you want to achieve.

Flooring and Carpet Options

I own a pair of shoes that I only wear to trade shows. They were really expensive, are fairly stylish, and are extremely comfortable, yet my feet still hurt at the end of each day. Good carpeting and padding increase your booth staffers' comfort. Just be careful not to get too much because a too-soft floor makes it worse, like walking on sand.

Trade show flooring also helps to give dimension to your display by defining your booth space. Modern printing techniques also make carpets with company logos quite affordable. Many exhibitors choose to use their flooring to clearly differentiate their booth from neighboring areas.

Counter and Pedestal Varieties

Counters are a vital tool for displaying physical products and promotional items and for lead-capturing devices. Depending on the booth size, counters can also be used as a reception area, where you can direct attendees to the appropriate area of your display. The options are up to you.

Some counters can have graphics wrapped around them, while others make a statement through their color and usage. A great benefit is that many counters have storage space, often with a lock and key to secure the items.

 In Chapter 6 of the CD, you will find the counters and pedestals color image.

Counter and pedestal display example.

(Sample image provided by Expodepot.com)

Literature Racks

Collateral and giveaways are the only things attendees will take home with them. The primary goal of your trade show literature is to provide information. Many literature stands look skimpy and seem to belong in a convenience store rather than a trade show booth. The most attractive literature holders have simple, modern designs. They should also be sturdy enough to resist bumps and vibrations common on show floors.

 In Chapter 6 of the CD, you will find a literature rack color image.

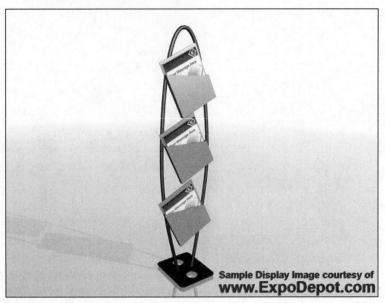

Literature rack display example.

(Sample image provided by Expodepot.com)

Table Covers

If you are exhibiting at a table top event, you have to make every inch of your display count. A significant part of your display is the cover of your table. Very much like pipe and drape sets, show-provided covers are often hideous yet are an important part of the display. Because of this, you should get your own table throw.

The numerous options available fall into two main categories: the traditional table cover, which is like a tasteful tablecloth, or the modern table cover, often printed with graphics. You need to pick color and logo options that complement your corporate look and that don't distract from the rest of your display.

 In Chapter 6 of the CD, you will find a table cover color image.

Table cover example.

(Sample image provided by Expodepot.com)

Lighting Options

There are a couple of great lighting choices that can be used on a trade show booth or display. Many display types come with lighting or provide options to add it. Almost every booth will need lighting to get the full impact of the displays. Lighting is a great, low-cost way to make your booth stand out.

Rental Displays Offer Benefits

Historically, exhibitors' most likely experience with rentals was as a last-resort option when their own display didn't arrive, or if they suddenly needed to simultaneously exhibit at overlapping shows. This is not surprising because, in the old days, rental offerings were very basic, were not terribly attractive, and did not offer exhibitors many opportunities to accurately portray their company's image. Things have changed quite a bit since then. Rental offerings are now stylish and customizable, offering wide varieties of creative options. New digital printing and manufacturing processes mean that exhibitors can design rental displays to accurately depict the style and branding of their company. Those technical improvements have been the driving force behind the rental display's transformation and have dramatically increased usage. Vendors now often have entire divisions dedicated to rentals and have warehouses full of options.

The Least You Need to Know

◆ Portability might be a key factor in deciding on a display type. Some you can transport yourself, while others need cargo crates.

◆ Depending on your situation, renting a display can be a smart choice, especially if you are exhibiting for the first time or need a second display.

◆ Certain display systems allow you to modify, grow, or adjust your display with relatively little additional cost.

◆ A number of money-saving options, such as used displays or simple displays, can get good results without breaking the bank.

◆ Kiosks are a great way to add functionality and sophistication to your booth.

◆ Lighting is a powerful tool that you should use to emphasize your booth or specific parts of it.

Chapter 7

Getting the Display Built

In This Chapter

♦ Decide what type of display vendor works for you and how your selection affects your ability to grow with a display

♦ Discover what is important to consider when selecting a vendor so that this complex task is well planned and executed

♦ Environmentally friendly exhibiting is a growing trend that should not be ignored

♦ Learn how to work with the selected vendors to get the display you need

♦ Discover the various phases involved in getting a custom display built

Main Types of Display Vendors

Whether your trade show program is large or small, unless you plan to sit on an empty floor, you need a display vendor to create the structure that will display your company's branding, messaging, and image to attendees. These companies are experts that are trained and experienced in the overall process of designing and producing exhibits from simple table top displays to custom-built booths from scratch.

There are a variety of vendors you can turn to for building your display, and each brings its own unique qualities and skill sets to the table. Finding the type of vendor best suited to your needs is key.

Show Smarts

If you are completely new to trade show exhibiting, consider attending a local trade show and looking at the various display types used. It should be a sizeable show, though, and not a table top expo.

Considering the type of display you are most interested in, while keeping in mind any financial constraints, you have two main directions to choose from. The first path leads you to a portable display vendor or marketing company focused on portable display needs. The second path leads you to a complete service display vendor that creates custom displays.

Portable Display Vendors

A portable display vendor is a vendor that specializes in easy-to-transport displays. A vendor in this category typically has access to products and accessories for all booth sizes, but its primary focus is on displays for 10'×10' and 10'×20' booths. Some carry only limited product lines, whereas others distribute just about every type of display, banner stand, and accessory on the market.

Vendors of this type offer great pricing because of their direct relationships with product suppliers. This attractive pricing benefits the customer. There are too many different vendors out there to describe the actual services each one offers, but the better display vendors take whatever time is necessary to learn about your objectives and what activities you plan in the booth. Then they make some suggestions that help you meet your needs and stay within your budget. If a vendor doesn't seem to be interested in learning about your needs and requirements and instead wants to focus only on your budget, consider that a warning sign and look for a different vendor.

Marketing and Advertising Companies

Because most marketing companies don't handle trade shows on a day-to-day basis but provide services all over the map—including web development, corporate identity, advertising, product packaging, and graphic design—they offer you a well-rounded package that covers more than just the display. They help you create a cohesive image, not only for your display but also for your collateral, presentations, promotional items, and accessories.

They can help you develop a complete theme for your entire exhibiting experience, although typically at a higher cost, especially as far as the display is concerned. Marketing companies usually purchase the displays from a regular display vendor and then mark the product up. My advice would be to look for a marketing company that handles many trade shows. They negotiate better prices for display items with their vendors and usually pass some of those savings on to clients.

Complete Service Display Vendors

A complete service display vendor can take a design idea written on a napkin and turn it into an impressive display by mixing various elements and materials together to create the best possible end result. These companies usually provide a lot of hand-holding and start by learning everything important about your industry, your company's objectives and trade show goals, what you plan to do in the booth, as well as the type and number of shows you plan to exhibit at.

Based on all that, a couple of concepts and themes will start coming together, and depending on your budget and design needs, they provide you with a variety of renderings of booth configurations and styles. These companies usually build larger displays for companies with larger budgets. The services are highly individualized for each client; you won't find "off-the-shelf" solutions from these companies. Everything they do is designed to make your display unique so that it stands out at a show.

"Green Exhibiting" Offerings

The world is becoming increasingly aware of the need to be more environmentally conscious. The trade show industry is jumping on the same bandwagon with a significant trend toward "green exhibiting." This is not just a trendy thing to do; it can make a very positive contribution to preserving natural resources and protecting the environment.

Entire "green displays" and accessories are now readily available and not just from companies specializing in these options. Most vendors have added green displays to their line, and if you are in the market for a new display that you plan to use for several years, you should consider an environmentally friendly display because you can expect attendees' feelings toward environmentally friendly exhibiting to become more common.

Green Exhibiting Goals

If you're considering a green display, you should make a list of your top environmental goals so that you can better compare vendors and their offerings. If your company already has green initiatives, get all the details and see how your trade show exhibiting can fit in. Chances are, you do not want to just have a display-building process that reduces air pollution or uses recycled materials. You want to use those facts in conjunction with how you present your company and your company's values. Essentially, create a list of what your environmental goals are.

Green Exhibiting Questions to Ask Vendors

Now that you have identified your environmental goals, you need to know what questions to ask vendors about their "green products." Here is a list of questions to help get you started. Customize these and add to the list based on your company's needs and policies.

- ◆ What type of energy-efficient lighting options do you provide?
- ◆ What type of fabric is used (if that is a factor in the display you are considering)?
- ◆ What type of carpeting and padding do you offer?

- Do you print with "green ink," and what does it consist of?

- Do you use wood in your display? (If the display has wood in it, ask what type of wood it is and what alternate options they provide.)

- Do you use recycled metal?

- What other recycled materials are used in the display?

- Is the manufacturing process for building the display energy efficient? Please describe how.

- Does your facility/office practice "green behaviors?" What are they?

- Does the display contain harmful or toxic ingredients?

Budget Savers
While a "green" booth is certainly not the cheapest option, the trend toward environmentally friendly exhibiting is gaining momentum. If you think your company will make use of an environmentally friendly image in the near future, it is cheaper to buy a "green" booth now than to buy a traditional one now and then a "green" booth two years down the road.

Display Vendor Type to Look For

As we all know by now, exhibiting at trade shows and conventions is not an easy task. So even when looking for a simple portable display, finding a company that provides management, inventory, shipping, and other services can be a smart move. Even if you don't need all those services right now, you might need them later on, and having a vendor that supports the growth of your exhibit program and understands your company's needs can be beneficial in the long run.

In today's Internet-based world, finding a display online is probably the cheapest way to go. Unfortunately, you often can't tell the quality of the company behind a given website until something happens with your display and there is nobody available to help you. So if you go the Internet route, try to find product reviews from customers before making your decision.

Look for reputable companies with physical locations in many cities or those with a network of affiliates that can help you out when an emergency arises in your exhibit city. For example, should your display not arrive, they will typically be able to provide rental options that are usually much cheaper than renting from the show. After all, you have an existing relationship with them.

Qualities of a Reputable Vendor

A good, reputable vendor cares first about the client's needs and the results the display produces. Of course, you can't tell this from the website or brochures, but it is noticeable during a more detailed conversation with the vendor. You should always spend some time talking to any potential vendor before making the decision to award your business. You should also look at the company's policies and procedures. The following are several items to pay attention to:

- Customer service availability and emergency contacts
- Dedicated account manager (preferable)
- Return guarantee within a specified timeframe
- Warranties—minimum 1 year or more
- Number of years in business, plus positive customer testimonials or references that are made available
- Thorough knowledge of the products and the trade show industry
- Product support for the lifetime of the product
- Trade show industry affiliations
- Name brand, quality products made of durable materials

Initial Vendor Research

Before you start searching for a vendor, you should know what you're looking for. You should also have a set budget (refer to Chapter 6). If you have a deadline, any vendor search has to fit within that timeline so you don't end up against the wall, forced to pick the only vendor that can deliver on time when you finally make a decision.

If you need three or four bids, you might have to speak with 10 or more vendors to find the companies you'd like more detailed information from. The following are several ideas that will help you find possible vendors:

◆ Search trade show industry websites, including trade organizations and associations.

◆ Read trade show industry publications such as *Exhibit City News* and *Exhibitor Magazine*, as well as e-mail newsletters, websites, and blogs.

◆ Ask for referrals from friends, colleagues, and former co-workers.

◆ Use online search engines like Google, Yahoo!, or MSN. Try a variety of very specific search phrases.

◆ If you work in a large organization, check to see if your company has an approved vendor list. This might make your choice really easy because you would probably have to use those vendors.

◆ Post a question in a trade show industry forum for feedback and referrals.

Once you have created a list of possible vendors, check out their websites for answers to initial questions by clicking through their pages, which vary by site. Some examples of pages might include services, products, FAQs, client testimonials, and designs. If you can't find the information you need on their websites, call them. Explain your needs and ask a few select prequalifying questions. During this phase, all you want to do is narrow down the list of candidates.

Evaluating Vendors

Once your list is down to about 10 companies, it's time to start more serious discussions with those vendors. Remember, the companies on your list should have answered the initial questions to your satisfaction.

Once you start talking in more detail with the vendors, it's easy to get overwhelmed by all the information being thrown at you. Always keep your list of criteria available and create a rating sheet to better compare the vendors. Have a clear definition of the type of company you want to do business with, and determine a rating system that helps you make an intelligent decision. Never ignore your gut feeling; if something doesn't feel right, there is often a reason. In that case, simply move on to the next prospect. Once you've narrowed down your list to about three vendors, it's time to request a formal proposal.

Request for Proposal

Now it's time to request a formal, written proposal. If you intend to work with a custom display company and you have many intricate details to consider, I suggest that you create a standardized request for proposal (RFP), which asks all bidders the same questions.

If you decide an RFP is the way to go, list all of the questions you want the vendors to answer and provide written instructions specifying the format for responses. Provide as much information as possible to potential vendors, such as timeline, budget, specific needs, desired reporting methods, and deadlines to be met.

> **Budget Savers**
>
> If you decide to use a complete RFP process, make sure you mark things as optional that you don't absolutely need. Otherwise everything you mention is factored into the quote, which may make your exhibit unnecessarily expensive.

Vendor Selection

If you have defined the selection criteria and ranked the answers of your final bidders, you probably have a favorite. As you move toward finalizing the deal, pay attention to details such as how easy the companies are to reach. If dealing with them is difficult before you buy, don't expect it to be any easier once you sign the deal.

Another thing to keep in mind is the potential value of a long-term relationship. If all you need is a one-time transaction, you can ignore that. But if you intend to purchase a display that you may keep or even add on to over the next few years, you should choose a company that you feel comfortable working with over a longer period of time. This is especially true if you have a complex, detail-oriented display. In that case you need a partner more than just a vendor, a supplier that has a truly vested interest in your success. I strongly advise against making price the deciding factor. Sure it's important, but remember: more often than not, you get what you pay for.

Customizing a Portable Display

Now that you have the company you want to work with for your portable display, it is time to focus on the specific services your company needs. If you selected a portable display unit and the various accessories you want off the shelf, you need to discuss the graphics and their placement. (See Chapter 8 for more information on graphics and messaging.)

Often the display company creates the design. However, if you want to use existing graphics or a third-party designer, you need to obtain the vendor's graphics requirements for your selected display. You also have to know the process for submitting graphics.

Once the graphics are complete, the vendor usually sets up the entire display with the graphics to ensure accuracy and a proper fit. One of the benefits of selecting a local vendor is that you can go and see the display for yourself. If that is not an option, the vendor can e-mail you a photo or post photos on a password-protected website.

Getting a Custom Display Built

Having a custom display built is similar to building a house. Your initial meetings with the custom display company are very much like meeting with an architect. You go through the information-gathering phase discussed previously. This helps your vendor understand the overall context of the project. Once the vendor has gathered all the necessary information, the design teams create concepts for both structural and graphic design.

Throughout this process you continue to see drawings and renderings, enabling you to make adjustments and approve various aspects of the design. In most cases, the display company will integrate your graphics directly into the design. This process usually includes scanning, image conversion, the creation of necessary graphics files, and the reproduction of your graphics, which includes printing, laminating, and finishing. It is common for the display company to work with your graphic designers or advertising agency to maintain a consistent look and feel across all aspects of your marketing activities.

Once all components are complete, your display is assembled in a staging environment to ensure accuracy and proper fit. After a quality-assurance cycle, your display is boxed and shipped to you or your show location.

> **Show Smarts**
>
> If you have a display custom built, ask if it can be built in a way that enables you to easily use components for a smaller booth.

Most custom display companies provide ongoing services such as installation, dismantling, regular maintenance work, reconfiguration, and storage between events.

The Least You Need to Know

- ◆ There are two main types of displays: those that are portable and those that require labor and professional installation for every show.

- ◆ Environmentally friendly exhibiting, called "green exhibiting," is gaining momentum, and you may want to consider those options as part of your display-selection process.

- ◆ When you look for possible display vendors, make sure you have a solid understanding of your needs so you can start soliciting proposals.

- ◆ Create a criteria list or even create an RFP document to solicit bids and compare vendors.

- ◆ Complete service vendors can be an asset if you want to build a long-term relationship; they can be very helpful in emergency situations.

Chapter 8

Displaying Your Message

In This Chapter

- ◆ How to develop targeted trade show signage
- ◆ Where to place marketing messages on your display items
- ◆ Simple marketing message formulas for everyone
- ◆ Creating graphics that will attract attention
- ◆ Using the right tools and file formats for the best results

Trade show environments only give you a second or two to attract attendees. Competing sights and sounds make this a challenging task. Having an attractive display with tight, targeted messaging and striking graphics is critical to the success of drawing prospects to your booth.

Compare this to visiting a shopping mall. If you are on your way to a particular store, additional stores you visit must have visual appeal and an attractive message, something as simple as, "Today only, 50 percent off all apparel!" Personally I like bargain hunting, so that message is relevant to me. Achieving relevance to prospects is a key task that your trade show signage and text have to achieve.

Trade show messaging is warfare, and the prospects' minds are under constant attack by competing messages. A trade show is hostile territory, with many conflicting messages reaching an attendee's mind. Simple-to-understand and relevant messages are important to winning this battle.

In this chapter, you learn how to appeal to your prospects' needs and build preference in their minds so that they will want to visit your booth for more information or buy your product on-site when allowed.

Compliance with Corporate Requirements

In most corporate environments, there is typically a specific branding and messaging style, often with precise wording, images, and taglines to follow. Familiarize yourself with all corporate guidelines and requirements before designing the display and messaging. Often there will be a style guide provided for you to follow.

Style guides change over time, and it is always a good idea to make sure you have the latest version. Sometimes you may find that your display no longer meets the requirements of an updated style guide, and you should find out if you have to change existing signage based on that. Though this goes beyond the scope of this book, depending on your role in the company, you may want to implement a style guide because it will help greatly to keep your marketing material looking and feeling consistent.

Branding Considerations

Even if you don't have a corporate style guide to follow, you will probably have branding considerations. Your company and products almost certainly have gone through some type of branding, whether accidentally or as part of a deliberate *brand management* exercise.

The idea behind branding is that you align the expectations customers have of your products with a brand experience, creating the impression that the brand associated with a product or service has certain qualities or characteristics that make it special or unique; in other words, it needs to make it better or more valuable in a prospect's mind. If you have brand management in place at your company, make sure your booth design and messaging complements the brand image your company has established. If you currently don't actively manage your brands, it might be worthwhile to add a book dedicated to that topic to your business book collection. For now, just keep in mind that any signage you create should be aligned with company branding.

> **def•i•ni•tion**
>
> **Brand management** is the application of certain marketing techniques to increase perceived value of a specific product or product line.

The Most Effective Message

Creating an effective message is not terribly difficult, but the concept is counterintuitive. Less is more, more is less. Human brains are trained to filter things out that are not relevant. The more information you expose someone to walking the aisles, the less likely his or her brain is to process all the information and bring it to the conscious mind.

Attendees process few words of your display and banner messaging before deciding to enter your booth or continue walking. Short, relevant benefit statement messages that are well aimed at your key prospects will draw them in. After you have them in the booth, you can expose them to more information. Having signage that is well targeted can also reduce the number of unqualified visitors. While that will limit the number of visitors to your booth, it makes sure you spend your booth time with the audience you want rather than large numbers of people who don't match your products or services.

Selecting Targeted Messaging

Picking the right message is not always easy. There may be several unique or interesting dimensions to a solution, but in the customer's mind there is a hierarchy of what matters. You have to aim for the top of that hierarchy. Only when you understand what motivates your customers to buy your product can you create messaging that is relevant to them.

Chapter 12 discusses how to identify your target prospects. If you are not familiar with your company's target markets and target prospects, you may want to skip ahead and read Chapter 12.

Product Benefits Are Keys to Success

Messaging needs to speak directly to prospects about how your product helps them solve a problem. That is what every purchasing decision is based on. Convey your product's benefits to attendees through the messaging on your display and banners.

To develop your messaging, I suggest you write a list of your product's benefits and then compare these with a list of problems your prospects experience. (These lists will also help you create messaging for other marketing items you will learn about in Chapter 10.) It is important to understand the distinction between *features* and *benefits*. Features may result in a benefit, but they don't belong on your main trade show signage.

def•i•ni•tion

Features are what your product does and how it functions. **Benefits** are how your product helps the customer.

A Simple Messaging Formula That Always Works

There is an easy messaging formula that can be used for any trade show signage, independent of the size of your company or who you are trying to attract. Don't be afraid to use this simple formula; professional marketing experts use templates all the time. Armed with information about your target market and the lists we covered earlier in this chapter, simply apply the following template. At the top of the banner, write "Ask Us How We Can Help You" followed by three benefit statements.

All you need is this message and a small logo on the banner. That's it. No phone numbers, website, or other unnecessary information cluttering it all up. Always remember: less *is* more.

Banner sample of simple messaging formula.

Corporate Users
Ask Us How We Can Help You...

**Get Rid of
Your Fax Server.**

- Unlimited Capacity

- Disaster Proof Redundancy

- Unparalleled Reliability

CONCORD

Budget Savers

Place the messaging on inexpensive banners, not on your large display. You may exhibit at a variety of shows with different target audiences where you need different messages to reach different prospects with different needs. This enables you to easily adjust the messaging without the expensive cost of replacing your main display.

Persuasive Messaging Words Influence Attendees

With an easy messaging formula to work with, adding persuasive words in your benefit statements will make the messaging appear more important to attendees. The following are 20 words marketers use to convince attendees to buy things or learn more about a product. Use these words to create interest in your booth and entice your target prospects to enter the booth and learn more about your product.

Discover how   Learn how

Easy   Increase

Eliminate	Free
Guaranteed	Simplify
Instantly	Reduce
Save	Take advantage
Solve	Accomplish
Exclusive	Improve
Satisfy	Techniques
Proven	Find out

Image and Graphics Style Considerations

Images and graphics stylize your display to portray the company image. Whether you want to appear fun, conservative, trustworthy, innovative, environmentally friendly, cost efficient, or whatever your image might be, graphics can get your company's image across to attendees and attract interest in visiting your booth. Use graphics to support and complement your company's messaging.

Like with the message itself, when choosing graphics, stick with simplicity. Be sure you don't select graphics that will contradict your carefully crafted message. Also keep in mind that whether you create your own graphics, have them custom designed, or select them from an image library, you need to follow the display vendor's graphics, file, and printing requirements.

Don't Do It!

A great example of contradicting messages and images is when politicians sometimes want to appear radically innovative and yet conservative at the same time to reach as many people as possible.

This doesn't generally work for politicians, and it won't work when combining your messaging and graphics. Don't use graphics that may contradict or question any of your messaging in the effort to reach more attendees. All this does is confuse attendees and make them walk past your booth instead of into it for a conversation.

Various Types of Graphic Elements

Photos are a widely used graphical element, but photos are far from being the only option you have when it comes to enhancing your display. What you need to find is a graphical element that accurately supports and represents the image you are looking to portray.

Here are some graphical elements to consider:

Show Smarts

When you design display graphics, remember that you are designing them for what *your prospects* are likely to be attracted to, not what *you* like or would be attracted to.

◆ Geometrical shapes

◆ Shading

◆ Texturized elements

◆ Cartoon characters

◆ Illustrations

◆ Hi-tech images

Finding Graphics and Images

There are many good sources for images that are either free to use or have a nominal *royalty fee* for use. A good source for royalty-free images is the clip-art library on the Microsoft Office website at www.microsoft.com. This site contains tens of thousands of graphics that can be used in your own designs and material.

def•i•ni•tion

A **royalty fee** (for these purposes) is the payment made for the use of an image, typically with a predetermined length of time or number of copies.

There are also a variety of websites, such as istockphoto.com, that provide professional images for a few dollars. Many software packages, such as photo-editing software, design software, or even web-development software, often come with image libraries that can also be used. If you are looking for image ideas, Google offers the capability to search for images. The images found are typically not available for licensing, but they can help you decide on a type of graphic to make it easier for you to search image libraries for a good fit.

> **Don't Do It!** ——————————————————
> Graphic design is an art form, and while it can be tempting to
> save money and work on the design yourself, this is an area best
> left to the experts unless you are either a great natural talent or have
> graphic design training. The design is an extremely important part of
> how your company and products are perceived, so be mindful of that
> when deciding between using a graphic designer or wielding the mouse
> yourself.

Targeted Design

A targeted design attracts your key prospects. One targeted design
option that prospects continue to respond positively to is using the
corporate logo's graphic element as the background, without any text
or the company name. Using the logo as a graphical element then
becomes the primary design aspect covering the entire display. If you
choose to go that route, make sure to implement this in complementary
corporate colors to maintain familiarity with your corporate identity.
This effortlessly combines the corporate look and branding in a clutter-
free design.

Whatever design elements you ultimately select to use, make sure you
maintain consistency. Carry the design's look and feel through to other
banners and items in the booth. If you don't, your booth will appear
disorganized in the minds of attendees.

The following image shows a sample of the large booth the same client
uses. They chose to use a 10'×10' pop-up display. As you can see, the
company name is easily visible, even when the booth is busy and people
are standing in front of it. This booth is designed to be simple, cost
effective, but bold. As mentioned earlier, the smaller banners provide
targeted information to attendees.

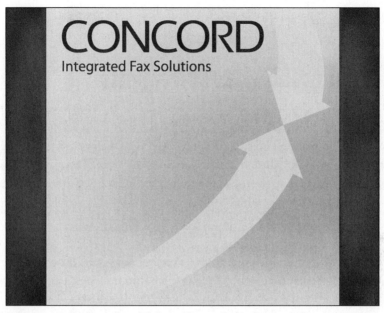

Banner sample of a targeted design using corporate logo and elements.

 On Chapter 8 of the CD, you can see the actual colors of this banner and several other client examples. For this image, the front is bright yellow with dark blue logo text—a can't-miss color with an easy-to-read logo. The darker blue areas are the sides of the banner; the fabric wraps around the sides.

Show Smarts

If you are working on your first trade show booth, enlist help to find a reputable vendor first. Vendors can advise you during the creation of your design. They can also assist with selecting the right software, file format, or a recommended designer if you prefer.

The Importance of Message Placement

When designing display graphics, what might look like a good design on your monitor may not even be seen once booth staffers and attendees fill up the booth. Make sure messaging or logo and tagline placement is at the top of the display, with a large, easy-to-read font that will be visible even when your booth space is busy and crowded. The best signage won't do you any good if it is hidden and nobody can see it.

General Graphics Requirements

Whether you create your own graphics, have them custom designed, or select them from an image library, you have to make sure that they can be reproduced in the size required. Much like you can't use a picture taken with your digital camera and enlarge it endlessly, the average graphic image can't withstand being enlarged to fit your display without looking fuzzy and grainy.

Any graphic you use should be vector based. Unlike raster graphics such as a photo, which become grainier the more you enlarge them, vector-based graphic files use geometrical relationships based on mathematical equations to represent images. This sounds more complicated than it is. Suffice it to say, use vector-based graphics because they can be enlarged indefinitely.

The following is a general graphics software and file guide you can follow. The most important thing is to make sure that whatever software you use can create the type of files your vendor accepts and uses.

♦ **Top recommended programs for creating graphics:** Adobe Illustrator 8.0 or higher and Adobe Photoshop 6.0 or higher.

♦ **Recommended file types for large-format printing:** Vector-based files created in Adobe Illustrator are always preferred, with a file format of EPS. Other accepted file formats are TIFF, PDF, or PSD (Adobe Photoshop file).

Color Modes

Files are typically converted to *CMYK* color mode before printing; select this as the color mode when setting up the artwork file. For an exact color match, select *PMS* (Pantone Matching System) as the color mode. There is typically an additional charge, but PMS colors will ensure color accuracy.

def•i•ni•tion

CMYK stands for cyan, magenta, yellow, and key color (black). **PMS** stands for Pantone Matching System. These are color modes as well as printing methods.

Type Guidelines

Not every vendor will have the carefully chosen type styles or fonts you used, and you don't want to have the font substituted with something different that throws off your entire design. While you can often send the font file to your vendor, it is better to use a file format where your fonts have been turned into outlines, such as in Adobe Illustrator.

In Adobe Photoshop, this is not relevant because the design becomes a TIFF, PDF, or PSD image file.

Giving Attendees More Product Information

Your trade show signage is the departure point for more information. Earlier in this chapter, we talked about the fact that your trade show signage has one purpose only: to attract the right audience to your booth. In order to achieve this, you have to minimize the information you convey.

Now that you have achieved that, you need to keep the attendees' attention and provide more information to complement the message on your display. Some of the most common items to offer include brochures, data sheets, flyers, case studies, press releases, and reprinted articles. Chapter 10 discusses these collateral items in further detail. Keep in mind, however, that any and all messaging vehicles need to be consistent with the core message on the display and follow the style and branding you developed to create a common look and feel that creates a complete picture of your products and services.

The Least You Need to Know

◆ Target messaging to your prospects' wants and needs through benefit statement messages that can be placed on smaller banners so you can inexpensively change messages based on the show type, industry, and audience.

- The best messaging won't do you any good unless people passing by your booth can read it. Make sure you never have messaging in areas that are likely to be behind attendees or booth staffers once the booth gets busy.

- Keep your display messaging and graphics simple and clutter free.

- At the top of your main display, only have your logo and tagline; no additional information is needed.

- The preferred graphic file type is a vector-based EPS. It can be enlarged indefinitely and will always look well defined, clear, and crisp when the artwork is printed.

Chapter 9

Booth Staff

In This Chapter

- ◆ Selecting the most appropriate booth staff
- ◆ Creating a booth staff training program
- ◆ Training booth staff to interact with attendees
- ◆ Teaching skills to booth staff through role-playing
- ◆ Booth staff responsibilities and commitments

Your booth staff plays one of the most important roles in forming an opinion about your company in the minds of attendees. No matter how well you have organized everything else, your booth staff, their behavior, and their techniques will be the single biggest factor in making the show a success or a failure.

You need to make sure your booth staff understands that physical appearance, choice of words, general demeanor, and their level of knowledge and enthusiasm are what determines the impression attendees will have of your company. This chapter will guide you through your booth staff selection and how to enable your staffers to be successful.

Selecting Booth Staff

The ideal booth staffer is a people person who is knowledgeable about your products and services, has high energy, is enthusiastic about your company, and is good salesperson. Odds are, most of your employees or co-workers will have some of these traits, but rarely will they have all of them. As a result, you may need to create shifts of people who have all those skills and talents in a combined form.

Booth Staff Responsibilities and Commitments

Being a booth staffer is an important contribution to the company's success and should not be taken lightly. The company sends employees to a show to meet new prospects, generate leads, and achieve other show goals. The company does not send them on a vacation to check out a new city or to find out which employee can drink or eat the most.

All booth staffers must be committed to maximizing the benefits of the show, willing to stay past the published show hours, committed to attending networking events outside of the show hours, and able to represent the company during any hour of the day.

Booth Duty

Because you carefully select staffers who best complement each other's skills for each booth shift, it is important that each booth staffer keep a schedule, arrive prepared, and arrive sufficiently rested. Stress the importance of not switching schedules with another staffer. If someone has a conflict, ask him or her to come to you personally, evaluate the importance of the request, and determine if alternate arrangements can be made.

It is also important to hold staffers accountable for being on time and following the dress code. It might be a good idea to offer some incentives such as gift cards awarded after the show for all booth staffers who meet their commitments. Let them know ahead of time you plan to reward those who do.

Networking and Prearranging Business Meetings

Because a trade show is typically much more than just a couple of show hours a day, it is important that booth staff members understand the requirement to attend networking events and other activities.

Sales staff at the show should have prearranged meetings with existing customers and prospects. If an attendee list is available before the show, or if preshow networking portals are available, make sure the sales organization makes use of these items early enough to set up as many meetings with prospects as possible. Have the sales team update you with its schedule before the show and during the show so you can keep track of where everyone is at any given time. Have a master schedule with everyone's meetings, the booth staff schedule, networking events, seminars anyone has requested to attend, and other activities.

Wearing a Uniform and Other Attire

You need to define a dress code for your booth staffers. Depending on the business you are in, this might simply be a business suit in a pre-defined color. Consider also having a nice, formal name tag with the company's logo and staffer's name, or a pin with the company's logo to wear with the suit. This adds a classy, professional touch and makes a subtle statement about your company's attention to detail.

More commonly, the show uniform is a shirt with the company logo and pants or skirts in a specific color. Keep in mind that logo shirt offerings vary significantly. Don't settle for the cheapest option. Spend time researching options with a quality vendor, and select a style that expresses the image of your company.

Show Smarts

You probably know most of the booth staffers well, so if you think it is necessary, don't be shy about mentioning upfront that white socks don't go well with the black slacks they are told to wear!

Observing Etiquette and Travel and Entertainment Guidelines

It should be obvious that general civilized behavior is expected at all times. Remind your booth staffers that being in the trade show booth is similar to being on a stage where the eyes of both attendees and the media are constantly on them, watching their behavior and forming opinions about your company. The same, of course, applies to networking events and private meetings with clients. If alcohol is served, make sure consumption is moderate. It is much easier and faster to destroy a good reputation than to build one.

Your company may already have travel and entertainment guidelines that apply to trade shows. If not, you should set guidelines so that all your booth staffers know ahead of time what is expected of them, what the company will pay for, how travel will be arranged, and what, if any, their individual budgets will be.

Training Booth Staff Before the Show

Booth staff training is important to the success of the event. There is no such thing as too much booth training, nor is there any employee who knows it all. You should either hire an outside consultant to conduct this training or develop your own training program. In either case, the training needs to prepare your staffers to sell and function in a trade show environment, which has competing sights and sounds. Essentially booth staff training needs to cover all the points made in this chapter.

Role playing is an effective way of practicing those techniques and can lead to more comfortable and confident members of your trade show team. If at all possible, organize several role-playing sessions and plan for staff members who are scheduled to work the booth together for the same role-playing sessions. This not only makes sure that everyone can attend, the repetition also helps your booth staff overcome initial shyness often associated with such an activity.

Show Smarts _____

Sometimes booth staffers, especially the ones who consider themselves veterans, may be a little opposed to the idea of booth staff training, claiming that they have been doing trade shows for years and know everything there is to know. Make sure they understand that they are required to attend and participate in sessions. Ask if they can help you by training and mentoring new staffers. This usually appeases them and makes them happier to participate.

Sharing Planning Details with Booth Staff

For some strange reason, trade show planning details are not often shared with booth staff, as if the plans are a secret to be kept sealed and tightly under wraps. Often booth staff members are just given their booth duty hours, times for networking events, and locations of shows.

If you follow the tips in this book, you should be proud of your show plan; share it with the rest of your booth team. It is much easier for them to work toward the company goals if they know what they are, understand what the company is investing, and grasp how important the results are to the show ROI and company revenue. Let them know what marketing programs are in place to attract visitors, what materials are being created, and what will be available at the event.

Describe Show Goals and Objectives

Part of your booth staff training is making sure all staffers understand what the goals and objectives are. Teach them what key messages are to be conveyed and outline the overall show strategy. Assuming you have goals for qualified leads for the show, break that information down into details that are meaningful to booth staffers. They should know that the goal might be to collect 400 qualified leads during the show, but they should also know that this translates into 15 qualified leads per booth staffer in each shift. Express your goals in a tangible way.

Describe Booth Layout

Unless your display got lost in transit and you had to rent one as an emergency measure at the last minute, a booth staffer should never be surprised by the layout and functions of your booth. If your exhibit is large, make sure everyone knows where specific demonstration stations are located; where lead collection devices are; and where to find collateral, supplies, and press kits. You should also explain any signage you have selected. Finally, show staffers a map of the show so that they become familiar with the show floor and your booth's location in relation to bathroom facilities, concession stands, entrances, and so on.

Media Procedures to Follow

Explain the media process to all booth staffers; they may feel confident and knowledgeable enough to talk to the media. Explain that even correct information can be presented or understood incorrectly and can lead to poor or negative coverage. Only individuals who have received media training should work with the media. Make sure everyone knows who the spokesperson is and instruct booth staffers to hand out media kits, collect business cards, and ask for a local number or cell number so that the company's media representative can schedule a meeting time if he or she is unavailable at that moment.

Interacting with Attendees

Knowing how to interact with attendees is an important skill that booth staffers must be able to master. They may be surprised to learn how many show attendees feel shy about approaching booth staff to ask questions. Teach your team how to use this fact to their advantage, and use the skills from this section to build on your booth staff training program if you will train internally.

Teach them to actively engage attendees who show interest in your booth while walking by and not to wait for attendees to walk in.

Show Smarts

With the combination of personalities assembled for booth duty hours, you should consider having booth staffers work the same shifts and learn how to work the booth as a team.

Use a staffer with an outgoing personality to act as a greeter and to get attendees excited and comfortable with entering the booth. This type of person will find this task easy to perform and will do it in a way that is engaging and entertaining to attendees. Then he or she can pass the attendee off to be further engaged and qualified by the staffer who he or she feels will match this prospect's personality the closest.

Engaging and Qualifying Prospects

Through training, your staffers will learn how to interact with attendees gracefully and make them feel comfortable in your booth. Staffers need to make their conversations warm and inviting and give the prospect a reason to stay. This is accomplished by knowing what type of questions to ask, making the conversation focused on the prospect's needs, and following the 80/20 rule: staffers should be listening 80 percent of the time and talking 20 percent of the time. It's important to allow prospects to open up and start talking about their product needs, what their work involves, and their decision-making power.

Staffers should draw from this data to gauge whether a prospect is qualified and how much time to devote to him. Staffers also must make sure to gather complete lead data and know what the most critical information to gather is so that the sales team can effectively follow up with prospects.

Asking Open-Ended Questions

To truly understand what an attendee is looking for, booth staffers have to ask open-ended questions. These questions require more than a "yes" or "no" answer to get prospects to explain what their needs and problems are so that staffers can properly qualify them. The following are some sample open-ended questions to use. Customize them to your company's specific needs and use them during role-playing exercises so that staffers become comfortable with using these types of questions in conversations to draw information from attendees.

- ◆ "Hello, what are you looking for in [specify product]?"
- ◆ "What about our exhibit caught your eye?"
- ◆ "What information can I tell you about our [xyz product]?"
- ◆ "Tell me more about your business ...."
- ◆ "What line of business are you in?"
- ◆ "What type of clients do you have and/or serve?"
- ◆ "How is your business marketed?"

 You will find a file concerning asking open-ended questions in the booth in Chapter 9 on the CD.

Disengaging from Unqualified Prospects

As important as it is to engage attendees, learning how to disengage from unqualified attendees ranks just as high. Staffers need to use the limited show time available for finding the next possible prospect, not staying in a conversation because they don't know how to end it.

They may feel a little awkward at first when dismissing someone. But if the attendee has no need for your product, there is really little point in wasting your staffer's time or the attendee's time. Once they have done it a couple of times, staffers will be much more comfortable and effective, and it will become second nature. The following phrases will help them make an exit as easy as possible. As with the previous questions, customize them to your business and have staffers practice them in role-playing activities during training sessions.

- ◆ "Based on our discussion today, unfortunately it doesn't sound like our company can help you at this time. Thank you for stopping by our booth; here's our website in case we can be of service in the future." (Hand them a business card or other inexpensive literature containing the website address.)

- ◆ "Thank you for this opportunity to talk today …."

- ◆ "I think I've taken enough of your time today …."

- ◆ "Thank you for stopping by our booth …."

When using these polite disengagement phrases, tell staffers to give the attendee a handshake to symbolize a courteous good-bye, and explain whether to hand the person an inexpensive piece of collateral or a "giveaway" item.

 In Chapter 9 of the CD, you will find a information on how to disengage from unqualified prospects.

Gathering Leads and Conveying Follow-Up Process

Describe to staffers that once a prospect has been qualified and all his or her questions have been answered, it is time to "close" him or her. Using the selected lead system (see Chapter 13 for more information about lead process), have staffers collect contact information and data about specific needs such as purchasing timeframe, purchasing authority, etc.

Have staffers describe the follow-up process and give a handshake before the prospect leaves the booth. After he or she leaves, the staffer should add notes from their conversation; this can be done as they speak to an attendee or after the attendee leaves the booth. If another attendee comes along before the staffer has a chance to write down notes, have her write the notes as soon as she can, while the information is still fresh in her head. The notes and data collected will help the staffer send the appropriate material after the show and will enable the salesperson to adequately prepare before calling the prospect.

Bad Booth Behaviors to Avoid

Remind your booth staff members that they have eyes on them at all times during a trade show, from prospects, competitors, media, photographers from the show, and even individuals with cameras. Don't let your booth staff get caught conducting the following bad booth behaviors, which I have termed "booth crimes." Add to this list to customize to your company policies.

The following is a list of the top 15 "booth crimes" to avoid while staffing your booth:

- ◆ Don't leave the booth unattended.

- ◆ No sitting, eating, or drinking.

- ◆ Limit alcoholic beverages during show floor receptions and networking events. It is unprofessional to be drunk and can ruin your company's reputation in the minds of certain attendees.

- ◆ No negative body language such as slouching, yawning, or crossing arms.

- ◆ Don't put a table in front of the booth; you want to draw attendees into the booth.

- ◆ No offensive odors; if a staffer is a smoker, he must always wash hands thoroughly and freshen up his breath after smoking.

- Always smile and look at a prospect you are speaking with; don't look over his or her shoulder for a better one. Disengaging the conversation is more professional if you find the person is an unqualified prospect.

- Don't get involved in long conversations with fellow booth staffers; stay focused on prospects. If a prospect sees you already involved in a conversation, he or she may walk past the booth.

- Don't spread rumors or make negative comments about competitors. Point out that you both offer good products; however, the benefits of your product are [start mentioning competitive advantages].

- Don't talk or text on cell phones in the booth; they should be put away during booth duty hours.

- Do not chew gum.

- Don't be late for a booth shift.

- Don't let the booth get disorderly and unorganized; look around the booth often, organize the booth, and throw away any garbage.

- Don't offend by telling off-color jokes or cursing.

- If there is something you are unsure of, try to find the right answer from a fellow booth staffer or tell the prospect you will follow up with him or her. Never make something up.

 Chapter 9 of the CD provides you with more information on bad booth behaviors to avoid.

How to Create Networking Superstars

You have already discussed with booth staff that there is much more to a trade show than just the floor hours. Explain that another, often almost equally important, part of the show is networking events. They provide a tremendous opportunity to meet potential prospects and business partners in an environment that is designed to build relationships.

Expect some pushback from some of your staffers along the lines of, "Why do I need to learn how to network? I go to events, shake hands, chat a bit, and get a business card." Well, wrong. During this part of booth staff training, explain that you will be teaching a strategic approach to networking that each staffer is expected to follow. The goal will not be collecting the most business cards but building a network of relationships that turn into referral machines and open doors for new business opportunities.

Dress for Success

The appropriate dress code may vary for each event, and the way staffers look is an important contributing factor to their success. Provide your booth staffers with a dress code for each event you want them to go to.

Bring Your Networking Tools

There is a small toolkit that every networker should have. It includes a name badge, business cards, and business cards of your company spokesperson in the event of meeting media contacts. Booth staffers who are not in a sales-related job function also can benefit from having a couple of business cards of salespeople with them.

Finding Trade Show Networking Events

Start looking for networking events well before the show starts. Frequently, the show's website will have a section dedicated to networking events and parties. When you are at the show, make sure to look in the show guide for any additional events. Be sure to add the events you want your show staffers to attend to their respective calendars or schedules. Lastly, be on the lookout for exhibit-sponsored events. You may receive invitations by mail or get them at exhibitor booths during the show.

Selecting Targeted Networking Events and Key Contacts

You have meticulously planned all the details of the trade show well in advance. Doing the same for networking events is a logical step. Create a networking plan and strategy that enables staffers to reach key contacts by attending targeted events, just like your company exhibits at targeted trade shows. Most evenings will have more than one networking event going on, so consider each one carefully and try to figure out who will attend which event and which event is most likely to provide an opportunity to build the relationships you are looking for.

After you have selected targeted events for staffers to attend, have them review the event and create a list of people they would like to meet and build relationships with. This doesn't need to be a list of actual names; it can be general terms such as company names, job titles, or just industry types. Having a clear idea who they want to network with will make it easier to react accordingly when the opportunity arises.

Also remind staffers that meetings can happen anywhere in a trade show environment. It starts with the breakfast buffet line and includes cab lines or shuttle buses. People tend to be very open to meeting new contacts at those places, and it is always a good idea for staffers to introduce themselves and learn more about the people around them. You never know who may turn out to be a potential prospect or new business partner.

Interacting with Networking Attendees

Teach your trade show staffers to introduce themselves. Don't have them wait around for someone to walk up to them. It's a networking event, not a place to get free food. Some of your team members, especially the ones not in a sales or marketing function, might be nervous about networking events. It may help them to team up with a more outgoing networking "buddy" who can start introductions for them and then move on.

Conversation Starters, Open-Ended Questions, and Discussions

Here is a list of 10 open-ended questions your booth staffers can use with attendees at networking events. Use this as a guide to get started; add more questions specific to your business and industry.

1. What does your company do?

2. What industry or industries does it serve?

3. Who are your key prospects/clients?

4. What types of products (and/or services) do you offer?

5. What makes you different from your competitors?

6. What got you started in this industry?

7. What do you enjoy most about your job?

8. What trends do you foresee in your industry segment?

9. What marketing/sales activities have you found to be most successful for your business?

10. Can you refer me to someone that does ___?

 Chapter 9 of the CD contains more information on conversation starters and open-ended questions for networking.

After initial introductions and learning a little about the new acquaintance, your staffers should have enough information to start executing their networking plan, meaning they will either start steering the conversation toward meeting their networking goals with that contact, or they will determine to move on to the next person.

Asking for Referrals

Have booth staffers prepare questions they can ask attendees at the networking event for specific types of referrals. Most people are happy to help and make introductions. Here are a few examples they can start with:

♦ Is there anyone here you can refer me to who needs a _____ type of product (service)?

♦ I'm hoping to meet with _____. Can you point me in the right direction?

♦ Can you suggest people I can speak with about _____?

♦ One of my goals for today is to meet someone who does/supplies (_____). Do you know of anyone here who fits that description? Can you introduce me?

Show Smarts

Create a pocket-size conversation cheat sheet for your trade show team members so that they have an easy way to look up and memorize the top phrases.

You can find more detail on asking for referrals in Chapter 9 of the CD.

Practicing Conversations by Role Playing

Just like the role-playing exercises for dealing with attendees at the show booth, develop role-playing exercises for networking events. This not only will ensure that everyone learns the right techniques, but will also make the less confident individuals feel more comfortable with their roles in the networking arena.

Evaluating Contacts

Tell booth staffers to evaluate the people they make contact with. Have them ask themselves this simple question about the contact: "Can I help them, and can they help me?" If the answer to either part of this question is "yes," then tell them to go build a relationship with the contact!

Show Smarts

When considering whether a new contact is helpful, remember that the purpose of the relationship isn't merely to get his or her business—it's to get business from everyone he or she knows!

Building Relations with Qualified Contacts

Ask booth staffers to follow this general guide once they have identified the most valuable contacts to build relationships with:

◆ Learn more about each contact's business, products, and personal interests. Consider setting up an initial face-to-face or telephone appointment of 15 to 60 minutes.

- Further educate the contact about your company and its products or services, and gently probe for personal interests as well (as appropriate).

- Touch base often and get together in person whenever possible.

- After building a relationship and developing a level of trust, start introducing the contact to other people with mutual interests. In turn, most contacts are likely to do the same.

- When looking for referrals, vendor recommendations, and general business advice, staffers will be able turn to their newly expanded base of contacts!

Maintaining Relationships with Contacts

Remind booth staffers that part of building useful contacts is relationship maintenance. You can point out that just as it takes work to maintain personal relationships, maintaining business relationships is no different. Have them keep the following tips in mind so that contacts don't "break up" with them:

- Touch base often, particularly with the most valuable contacts. Go to lunch or dinner, attend an event together, or simply pick up the phone and chat a bit.

- Check in with all contacts periodically to maintain the relationship. Even a simple, quick e-mail or card will do the trick.

- Prioritize contacts every so often: as their contact base grows, staffers should evaluate which contacts they need to be in touch with frequently and which require attention just periodically.

Booth Staff Guide

For each show, create a customized "Booth Staff Guide" to serve as a reference tool when needed. It should contain all the relevant show details such as show hours with booth staff schedules, networking events, and who is assigned to attend them. In addition, include the show goals and objectives, the lead-handling process, and the travel arrangements and contact numbers for each team member. Adding the cheat sheets completes the guide.

The Least You Need to Know

♦ Develop and execute a comprehensive booth staff training program or bring a consultant in to help with training.

♦ Have all your booth staffers participate in multiple role-playing sessions to develop their booth and networking skills.

♦ Evaluate booth staffers and create teams with personality styles that complement each other to work the same booth staff shifts and learn how to work the booth as a team.

♦ Have each team member create a personal networking plan outlining specific networking events and networking goals.

♦ Provide a detailed "Booth Staff Guide" to each booth staffer for each show.

Part 3

Planning: Marketing and Sales

Just showing up at a trade show with a nice display and smiling booth staffers won't quite cut it. You're there to differentiate yourself from your competitors and to collect leads you can later turn into sales.

If you wanted to gamble, you would have gone to a casino. Instead, you should try to leave as little as possible to chance; this is why you develop a comprehensive trade show marketing plan that covers everything that will make you successful. The trade show marketing plan is the centerpiece of your trade show efforts and will guide you to a successful show execution.

Chapter 10

Your Trade Show Marketing Plan

In This Chapter

- ◆ Set goals and objectives for the show
- ◆ Plan marketing activities based on selected goals and objectives
- ◆ Choose collateral targeted at the attendees' needs
- ◆ Evaluate show-offered marketing opportunities

Your trade show marketing plan is the summary of all research you conducted and the conclusions and tasks you developed based on it. The marketing plan is not only a formal document that serves as a tool to develop your strategy, it is also a document that an outsider, such as an executive of your company who is not involved in planning the event, can use to understand the strategy and goals as they pertain to that particular event.

The trade show marketing plan functions like a mini business plan that is specific to an individual trade show or convention. It explains the reasons for your trade show actions, what resource requirements there are, and how they are to be met.

Developing Your Strategy

To develop an effective strategy for each show, you have to evaluate all the information you have gathered and create goals and tasks to create your trade show marketing plan. If you have the option, involve members of the marketing team or management team to validate and fine-tune the individual parts and goals of your strategy.

Reviewing Attendee Demographics and Target Prospects

The key to a successful strategy is a solid understanding of the attendee demographics and your target prospects, as well as your competitive position. Always keep in mind why you selected this show, what is included in your show package, and what your preliminary goals are (the ones you created in Chapter 2).

Familiarize yourself with the attendees' expectations and reasons for attending this show. Depending on who your target prospects are, they may have priorities and needs that change seasonally or that relate to external factors such as high energy costs or changes in legislation. Before proceeding with your marketing plan, make sure that any previously made assumptions regarding the attendees and your prospects are still unchanged.

Researching Competitors Exhibiting

Make a list of competitors who are registered or are likely to exhibit at the show. Your marketing plan should reference their profile and position in the market.

Research as much detail about their planned show activities as you can. The more detail you have the better. If you can, find out their booth size and the sponsorships they have signed up for, the private events they are planning, and the announcements you expect them to make. Use this information to differentiate yourself from your competitors by fine-tuning your *unique selling proposition (USP)*.

def•i•ni•tion

Your **unique selling proposition (USP)** is the description and points for how your product is different, or better, than your competitor's product.

Reasons for Selecting This Show

Reference notes on why you selected this show as a refresher, including what factors—such as attendee demographics, networking opportunities, and PR opportunities—contributed to that decision and how you weighted each of those factors.

If this show is part of a broader marketing strategy, reference what that part is and how this show fits in.

Primary Agenda for Attendees

List why attendees go to this particular event and what their expectations are. This will help you decide on marketing materials and pre-show marketing. This information can be gathered from the show prospectus and the show's website.

Every activity you add to your marketing plan needs to be based on what the attendees want and what they are interested in and care about, not what you want to do for the show because you or someone in the company likes it. The key to good trade show marketing is catering to the attendees' needs and expectations.

Set Goals and Objectives

Your trade show marketing plan needs to list measurable goals and objectives. Depending on your show's focus, your plan may not need to contain each of the areas discussed in the following sections. Select only the ones that apply to each trade show's individual marketing plan.

Start by explaining what products and services are showcased. Have a maximum of three goals in each of the sections that follow, and make sure they are realistic and obtainable. Having too many goals will not only dilute your focus, it virtually guarantees that you will not reach several of them. Keep in mind that, after the show, you will measure your success based on the goals you defined here.

Show Smarts _____

Many exhibitors at trade shows tend to "wing it"—just show up and see what happens. If you bought this book, you probably don't plan on doing that. You are actively creating strategies to improve your company's trade shows.

Keep those other exhibitors in mind. Some of them may even be competitors of yours. The more prepared you are when you show up to a trade show and the more efficient and effective your strategy and planning is, the better your position is to gain respect and attention from attendees and to gather more qualified leads.

In Chapter 10 on the CD, you will find more information about setting goals and objectives.

Products or Services

If your company has a large number of products and services, you have to select a limited number to focus on. Base your product selection on what attendees are most likely to be attracted to and need for their job functions.

The following is a list of possible goals and objectives you may decide on. Feel free to modify them or add your own. You may also want to mention in your trade show plan that these goals are based on return on objectives (ROO)—the type based on activities accomplished, not based on sales.

- ◆ Demonstrate benefits, data, or features of product(s) or service(s)

- ◆ Promote positive product or service trends

- ◆ Cross-promote services or product applications

- ◆ Be compared with other vendors or solutions

- ◆ Demonstrate improvements of product(s) or service(s)

- ◆ Showcase new product(s) or service(s)

Sales, Marketing, and Market Research

Your goals in this category should go beyond just creating a number of qualified leads, even though this might well be your primary focus. Discuss your objectives with other departments of the company, such as product management or your research and development group, to see if this show can help them with projects they are working on. Here is a list of possible goals to get you started.

◆ Position the company in the market

◆ Develop leads for the internal sales team

◆ Develop leads for partners

◆ Reach decision makers

◆ Create customer lists

◆ Uncover customer attitudes

◆ Introduce a new approach to the market

◆ Obtain feedback on a product/service

Networking

Networking is one area that will probably have fairly identical goals, at least conceptually, for every show you exhibit at. In most cases, just the numbers and quantities of contacts and activities will change from show to show. Here are some potential goals:

◆ Meet qualified contacts from the networking plan

◆ Build business relationships with qualified contacts

Public Relations

In most cases, your public relations focus will be specific to one of the following goals. However, there might be a need to adjust some of these based on the type of publications you are able to meet with. Here are some potential goals:

- Create and project an image

- Highlight new products or services to the media

- Showcase a particular side of the company

Measurable Objectives

End the goals and objectives section of your trade show marketing plan with quantifiable and measurable goals. These will define the key performance indicators to track, allowing you to measure the success of this particular event.

- Reach _____ number of decision makers at the show.

- Create more contacts per salesperson in a given time period; define a goal for a number of meetings 30/60/90 days after the show.

- Prearrange _____ number of at-show sales meetings per salesperson.

- Create more sales per salesperson in a given time period; define a goal for the number of sales closed in 30/60/90 days, within 1 year, and so on after the show. (Choose realistic goals based on your company's sales cycle process.)

- Collect a minimum total of leads.

- Collect a minimum total of qualified leads.

- Meet with _____ number of media contacts at the show.

- _____ number of articles published about the company after the show in targeted publications. (You may choose to include a list of publications.)

- Prearrange _____ number of meetings with media contacts from a predetermined list of industry publications.

Goal-Based Planning for Trade Show Marketing

Based on the goals you selected, you will have a variety of marketing options and techniques to help you meet them. Tables for each marketing timeframe in the upcoming sections of this chapter provide you with an overview of what marketing activities are most suitable for specific goals. You should have three or four sections in your trade show plan categorized by where and when you will execute planned marketing activities.

 Chapter 10 of the CD has more information on selecting marketing activities based on your goals and objectives.

Preshow Marketing

Preshow marketing activities create awareness, enticing prospects to plan a visit to your exhibit while at the show. Some activities include announcements that you will be at the show (including your booth number), direct mailers or e-mails to attendees, advertisements, and so on.

The following table describes preshow marketing activities and the various goals each activity might achieve.

Pre-Show Marketing

Item	Image Awareness	Product Introduction	Sales	Generate Leads	Preschedule Appointments	Media Attention
Advertise in trade publication	❏	❏	❏			
Advertise in direct e-mail	❏	❏		❏	❏	❏
Advertise in direct postal mail	❏	❏		❏	❏	
Advertise in press releases	❏	❏		❏	❏	❏
Advertise in telemarketing	❏	❏			❏	

Table created by TradeShow Teacher

At-Show Marketing

At-show marketing activities are the programs you run during the actual show and include items such as billboards at the airport, custom-printed room keys at show hotels, events you are organizing during the show, advertisements in the show guide, etc.

The following table describes at-show marketing activities and the various goals each activity delivers.

At-Show Marketing

Item	Image Awareness	Product Introduction	Sales	Generate Leads	Preschedule Appointments	Media Attention
Advertise in trade publication or show issue	❑	❑	❑	❑		
Airport advertisements	❑	❑				
Billboard advertisements	❑	❑				
Hospitality events	❑	❑				
Hotel T.V. advertisements in-room	❑	❑				
Promotions	❑	❑				
Mobile ads	❑	❑				
Press interviews	❑	❑				❑
Show daily advertisements	❑	❑	❑	❑		
Show directory advertisements	❑	❑	❑	❑		
Show hall ads/boards	❑	❑		❑		

T.V. and photo opportunities	❏	❏	❏

Table created by TradeShow Teacher

In-Booth Marketing

Marketing activities within the booth are designed to draw attention to your booth and get you more booth traffic. Be careful with these activities, though, because they can easily lead to nonqualifying attendees visiting your booth, which will reduce your percentage of qualified leads. This makes it more difficult and costly for your sales force to follow up.

The following table describes in-booth marketing activities and the various goals each activity delivers.

In-Booth Marketing

Item	Image Awareness	Product Introduction	Sales	Generate Leads	Preschedule Appointments	Media Attention
Celebrities				❏		
Contests, drawings, and/or games	❏			❏		
In-booth premiums				❏		
Live presentations and entertainers	❏			❏		

Table created by TradeShow Teacher

Postshow Follow-Up Marketing

There are a variety of postshow marketing activities you should consider. Show producers may make the attendee list available to you postshow, and you may want to follow up with direct mailers, e-mails, advertisements, or press releases mentioning awards you may have received at the show.

Postshow marketing activities should not be missed in your trade show plan; they offer one last shot at leveraging your exhibiting efforts from the show.

Show Smarts

Consider sending several postshow follow-up items, such as direct mail or e-mail, or consider advertisement in an industry publication, particularly one produced by the show. A great item is a general "thank you" to those who visited your booth and a "sorry we missed you" to those who weren't able to stop by.

Invite attendees to visit your website for more information. Consider offering an incentive for following up with a salesperson within a certain timeframe for more information about the company. Always make sure any ad you create includes several benefit statement messages (see Chapter 8).

Show-Offered Preshow Marketing Opportunities

In addition to your own preshow marketing activities, which were discussed previously, the show organizer will frequently offer preshow marketing opportunities, and some of them may be part of your package. Examples of this are direct mailers or e-mails sent to registered attendees, using content that you provide.

Using a Theme

While this isn't a specific goal you list in your goals section, it is certainly your objective to provide a well-rounded, comprehensive booth experience to all your visitors. A technique that can help with that is using a theme since it will help you stand out both on the show floor as well as in the minds of your attendees.

To achieve this, however, you have to make sure the theme carries through to everything relating to your booth—from the display to booth staff attire to colors and promotional items. Otherwise, your creativity will be overshadowed by the items that don't fit in or are missing.

Prospect-Targeted Collateral

Any collateral you decide to bring to the show or produce for it needs to be aimed at the prospects you are interested in. Depending on your audience, different types of collateral will make a bigger impact. Plan to bring the appropriate collateral items that will benefit your attendees the most and help you reach goals.

Case Studies

A case study takes your prospect on the journey of an actual user experience with your product. Included are examples of a customer's situation or problem before using your product followed by a description of how your product or service helped the customer.

This is a great tool to help attendees visualize how your product has already helped someone else with potentially familiar concerns and issues. Each case study should have a table or bullet point area that shows the features of your product that were instrumental in solving the client's problem.

Brochures

This is the one item that you will probably need to have in any exhibiting situation. Brochures are your company's front line in communicating your products and services in an easy-to-read format. Any brochure must emphasize the benefits of your products and services and should communicate to the reader why your offering will improve the prospect's situation.

> **Don't Do It!**
>
> When creating your brochure, don't focus on the features of your product; focus instead on the benefits users experience when using your product. Those are the items that help the person reading the brochure relate to the effectiveness of the product.
>
> A bunch of text with lists of features talking about the specific components of your product won't mean much to readers because they can't relate to those items. The primary goal for the brochure is to create interest; the follow-up conversation or materials requested can explain the features of the product.

Flyers

Flyers are often about the size of a postcard, but they can be larger and often contain some sort of promotion. Some shows will let you walk around and distribute flyers to attendees; this is a great form of *guerilla marketing* that provides a cheap way to draw people to your booth. However, check the show's rules and regulations first if you plan to distribute at the event. You may be restricted from doing so. Naturally, you can distribute them to attendees who visit your booth, and in many cases you can distribute flyers outside the exhibition hall (like on the sidewalk leading to the entrance).

def•i•ni•tion

> **Guerilla marketing** is a term coined by Jay Conrad Levinson to describe marketing that uses unconventional approaches to promote and attract interest in a product or company. Time and imagination are key components in guerilla marketing, not money. This is why entrepreneurs and small- to medium-sized businesses find these approaches appealing.

Data Sheets

If you have technical or complex information that you need to provide so prospects understand what you offer, then a data sheet is a great tool to use. Many industries use data sheets containing a mixture of benefits and features to describe a single technical product or service.

Often data sheets include technical diagrams or pictures to make complex information easier to understand. What makes data sheets a great tool at trade shows is their ability to inform visitors about certain details of your products or services without the visitor feeling required to start a detailed conversation. At the same time, your booth staff can observe which data sheets a visitor is looking at and then approach the attendee already knowing what products or services the visitor is interested in.

Article Reprints

If you have been mentioned or featured in a newspaper, magazine, or online publication, contact the publication to order reprints or to obtain permission to reprint the article yourself. Having a third party endorse your product or company is a persuasive way to gain the confidence of your prospects.

The Least You Need to Know

- ◆ Your trade show marketing plan is not only a tool to help you develop and articulate your show strategy, it is also the vehicle that helps nonmarketing members (such as senior management) understand what the goals of the show are and how they will be achieved.

- ◆ Set a few specific, measurable goals that you will use to evaluate the show's performance.

- ◆ Plan for appropriate marketing activities before, during, and after the show.

- ◆ Select the appropriate collateral to meet the needs of your target audience.

Chapter 11

Trade Show Public Relations Activities

In This Chapter

- ◆ Finding press release distribution outlets: free and paid
- ◆ Compelling the media to meet with you at trade shows
- ◆ Announcing newsworthy information
- ◆ Obtaining the contact information of attending media
- ◆ Creating publicity from speaking opportunities at trade shows

Positive media coverage of your company and products often has a much higher impact than paid advertising in the same publication. You probably know enough about advertising rates to understand that a good article has significant value.

A trade show environment provides you with the unique opportunity to meet a large number of media representatives face to face. It is much easier to get a couple minutes of a reporter's time during a show than at any other time. If you exhibit primarily within the same industry at multiple shows, you will find that many of the reporters are the same at each show, helping you to build relationships over time.

Hire a PR Firm or Plan Yourself

Unless you have significant PR experience within your company, hiring a public relations company for a couple of shows is a great way to watch and learn its techniques as it meets with reporters. If your budget allows such an expenditure, plan to have a PR agency manage your media activities for about four to six shows.

After these shows, you should have established relationships with most of the reporters covering your industry and obtained their contact information. This makes the incremental value of a PR agency decrease. Hiring a PR agency, however, is by no means a prerequisite for media success at trade shows. The simple techniques and tips in this chapter will show you how to achieve successful results when handling PR.

Press Release Announcement

As an exhibitor at a trade show, you need to publish a minimum of one press release. Even if no media outlet picks it up for an article, at a minimum it will show up on numerous websites that archive and list press releases, resulting in more links to your website and increased search rankings.

If you plan to announce a new or improved product or service, you have a great reason for a second announcement, which will have a noticeably higher impact than the first, as this is more interesting to the media and your company name is still familiar from the previous announcement.

> ### Show Smarts
>
> At a minimum, when exhibiting at a trade show, write a press release that includes the full official show name, the show's dates and location, and of course your booth number. It's always a good idea to mention the products and services you showcase and to list any possible incentives for visiting your booth.
>
> A simple announcement like this will not result in much if any media coverage, but its posting on the show's site results in increased keyword rankings on search engines and reminds media attending the event of your existence.

Announcing Seminar Presentations

If your company is presenting a seminar or panel discussion at the show, you have another great opportunity for media activity. It certainly warrants another press release, and you should invite media specifically to that event.

When sending a press release or pitch letter inviting media members to attend, list the most important items they will learn during the session to spark their interest. A session like this should also be announced within your own company, and sales and marketing should invite current and potential customers to attend. Mention the seminar on a company blog if you have one, and prominently announce it on your company website to support industry experience claims.

 You can find a press release template in Chapter 11 of the CD.

Press Release Distribution

There are many different ways to distribute press releases. The paid methods, such as using a wire service, produce better results and get more attention from the media. Wire services offer regional and/or national distribution as well as industry-specific distribution.

Free distribution sites get noticeably less attention from the media, but by posting your release on these sites, you get increased search rankings on the web. Last, a couple of industry publications now have their own web release submission portals. Make good use of those because often their editorial staff paraphrases parts of the submitted releases and uses those in their online and print editions.

Partner Websites

Whenever you announce any trade show–specific activities, especially if they involve awards or other specific accomplishments, always ask your business partners to publish it on their websites. If you have reseller channels, for example, they benefit directly from your product winning an award, and they should be motivated to help you spread the news.

Virtual Press Office

Shows frequently attempt to limit your direct access to the press section on their websites and instead offer a virtual press office or media networking portal. These sites often charge to post a release, but if your release is newsworthy, it is worth the relatively modest fees.

You can often post marketing materials here as well, which is similar to an electronic media kit. Media members are inclined to look at the information in the virtual press office (VPO) because the fees associated with it indicate a level of commitment from the exhibitor.

Media Room at the Show

Bigger shows have media rooms. You should have an ample supply of press kits available there. A typical press kit for a trade show contains the two or three most recent press releases, especially if any of them contain announcements of new products or services introduced at this show.

You should also have a couple data sheets or brochures, a biography of key executives and your company spokesperson, and a business card for the company's media contact. Beyond that, include any items that make the reporter's job of writing about your company easier, such as a CD that contains case studies.

Media Preparation

As with anything else related to organizing the trade show, your media activities should begin with detailed planning well ahead of the show. You need to define goals and a budget and then execute the plan you put together. Your first step should be to research the quantity and type of media expected at the event.

Request Attending Media Contact List

As an exhibitor, you should have access to a list of reporters attending the show. This list is maintained and provided by the show and tends to change significantly over time. Although you should get the list as early as possible, keep getting updated versions to contact individuals who have been added. The media list may even get updated during the event. Media attendees who get added to the list that late often have far fewer planned activities, so it is often easier to arrange a last-minute presentation or interview with those individuals.

Pitching Attending Media for Meetings

A lot of the legwork for successful media coverage is done in advance. Start contacting attending media members to set up meetings during the show the moment the first reporter is confirmed to attend.

You or your PR agency needs to set up as many media meetings as possible. To be successful at that, you have to develop a pitch that compels reporters to meet with you. Using case studies to support your claims and discussing industry trends or research you have done can entice the media to meet with you. Unless you work for a well-known brand, the fact that you have a new product is rarely enough to secure the meetings you want.

Pitching the Media to Review Your Product

Both before and during the show, you have opportunities to convince reporters to review your product. If you are launching a new product at the show, advance copies or versions can help get the attention of publications and reporters. Follow-up meetings at the show can then answer any questions they may have from testing your product or service.

More often, however, you'll find yourself pitching reviews of your product to the media during the meetings you set up at the show. If you are fortunate enough to have won some show award by the time you meet, be sure to capitalize on that third-party validation. Other than that, case studies and brand-name clients who are willing to be interviewed or to function as references are invaluable when it comes to convincing the media to cover your product.

Press Conferences

If your company or product announcement is important enough and you expect media interest to be greater than what you can handle in one-on-one meetings, consider holding a press conference. This enables you to address a larger crowd in a single event. Having a press conference for any other reason pretty much won't work.

One-on-one meetings help build relationships; press conferences don't. One-on-one meetings enable you to tailor your message to the publication's audience; press conferences don't. Never expect reporters who would not be willing to meet individually to show up at a press conference. Consequently, you should only hold a press conference if the number of reporters and the scheduling availability of company resources don't allow you to get your message across in individual meetings.

Plan Media-Only Exclusive Events

Unlike a press conference, which is successful only if you have enough clout to attract a large group of media professionals, organizing specific media events that provide additional incentives to attend can be a way for smaller, lesser-known organizations to assemble a sizable number of reporters.

Good venues for an event like this are locations that provide some type of tourist value to the attendee. River boat cruises, visiting a winery, a buffet meeting in a unique location, or a meeting at a major entertainment park (including, of course, the tickets to it) can greatly improve your chances of attracting reporters who are otherwise hard to reach. Do your research before planning such a costly event to avoid conflicts with events being held at the same time.

Seminars

As mentioned earlier in this chapter, seminars (or "speaking sessions" as they are often called during shows) are always a type of PR activity whether you have media present or exclusively address a public audience. Seminars are always a good way to increase the exposure of your company within an industry and lend an expert status to your company's speakers.

Free Seminar Presentation Opportunities

There are both free and paid speaking opportunities. You can't go wrong with free opportunities, though they tend to be much more restrictive about the topic you can cover. They focus on education and facts about industry trends, changes in technology, and so on.

That doesn't mean you can't mention your company name or products; it just means you have to be a little more skillful in weaving that information into your presentation. One easy way is to use your product or company as an example for an industry trend or change in technology. Doing this in an obvious manner, though, becomes a turn-off to attendees who are serious about learning new information.

Paid Seminar Presentation Opportunities

Paid sessions can be great marketing tools or expensive flops. I always feel bad for companies that spend significant amounts of money to speak during a buffet lunch, thinking they will get a lot of attendees to listen about their company and products, only to find that attendees are on the phone, checking e-mail, or chatting amongst themselves. Before signing up for any paid session, make sure you can attract the audience you want during a time when audience is willing and able to pay individualized attention to you.

Selecting a Company Speaker

Selecting the perfect company speaker is a little like selecting the perfect booth staffer. Look for someone who is not afraid to speak in front of a crowd; eloquent yet easy to understand; quick on his or her feet when it comes to thinking of good answers to questions; humorous; and knowledgeable about your industry, products, and company.

Most likely, you'll have to compromise on some of those traits, but being knowledgeable and coming across as confident and easy to understand are essential. If your company plans to set up speaking sessions at various industry shows, consider professional speaker training for the company's speaker to enhance his or her presentation skills and better represent your company.

Call for Speakers and Seminar Proposal

Show producers start selecting the seminar speakers at least nine months before the show. Keep in mind that the seminars are a big part of a show's appeal and are used heavily in preshow promotions. So to have a good shot at securing a free seminar opportunity, submit your proposal early. Call for speakers and submission deadlines should be easy to find on the show's website.

Show Smarts

Officially, speaker selections are based on expected public interest in their submission topics. In reality, however, it often depends on which companies exhibit often. Even if you haven't signed up to exhibit yet, explain to your show sales representative that you are not ready to commit to exhibiting until you know if your spokesperson will be needed at the show. You might be surprised how quickly your session ends up on the schedule.

Be Informational and Entertaining

Most likely, you also want your company to present at the next year's event. While many factors contribute to whom is selected, good reviews are important for repeat presenters. Most shows ask attendees to evaluate each seminar attended; good evaluations help secure a session the following year.

Attendees want to learn about your topic, so cover information that goes beyond average knowledge. At the same time, attendees want to enjoy the session and want to be entertained. Finding the right balance between dry facts and entertainment takes a little bit of experience and time; always ask for a copy of your evaluation results so that you can make the necessary corrections.

Best-of-Show Award

Almost every show has some type of best-of-show award. In most cases, there are multiple categories based on industry or application. Often there are categories for "Best New Product," "Best Small Business," "Best New Innovation," and many more.

If you have a relationship with the show's producer, suggest a new category that might make it easier for you to win an award. Most shows require you to submit your product or service for consideration well in advance of the show. Rules vary greatly from show to show, so make sure you understand them before making any submissions.

Show Smarts

Many companies don't bother submitting for a best-of-show award or overlook the opportunity. This obviously increases your odds of winning an award at that show. Some shows garner a great deal of submissions, but others have only a few. Outsiders don't know that, though. They are simply impressed with the fact that you won an award! The major point here is to look for award submission opportunities at every show you exhibit at.

Research the Show's Award Program

The first step, of course, is to research what award programs the show has. Most shows have some type of exhibitor awards, but not all of them do. This information can usually be found on the show's website.

If you have difficulty finding it, call the show's producer. Some shows have fees associated with award submissions, others allow only one submission per company, while others may allow you to submit all your products in every category offered. So your submission strategy varies greatly depending on the show's rules for its award program.

Select a Product for Submission

Unless there is neither a cost nor a limit on submissions, you want to consider carefully what product or service you submit and in what category. Many shows allow you to have one submission per category. In that case, create a matrix showing each category and what, if any, of your products might have the best chance of winning.

If you have to pay for submissions, you have to be even more selective about the product and category you choose. Look for categories that eliminate parts of your competition. Some shows have a category for products announced at the show, for a new product provided by small business, etc.

Award Submission

Award submission rules vary greatly. The only thing they have in common is deadlines. Most have restrictions on the number of words you can use to describe your product and its benefits.

Make sure you understand and comply with the rules and requirements. Submissions not following the rules are often immediately eliminated without any consideration of the submission, even if it is the most innovative product at the show. Don't ruin your chances of winning; just follow the rules.

Announcing a Best-of-Show Award

If your company, products, or services win a best-of-show award, react quickly to maximize the benefits. Have a press release template ready to go. After you win, send the release directly to the appropriate editors of your target publications and to attending media members, who will hopefully include your announcement along with their coverage of the show.

Media names and contact information for publications not at the show can be found on the publication's website and should be researched well in advance of the show. Most often, the show makes a press release announcement with a list of the winners. Like your other press releases related to the show, add your best-of-show release to the corporate website and any coverage the show distributes. Also release the announcement on paid and free press release sites. Because winning an award is a third-party validation of your product or service, don't forget to mention the award in collateral and marketing materials. Announce the win to existing customers and use it as a marketing touch point. Send an announcement to leads collected from trade shows that have not been turned into sales yet.

Show Smarts _____

Winning a product or best-of-show award is a huge accomplishment for your company; announcement and marketing opportunities should be maximized. When winning awards, you often receive a graphic created specifically for award winners to use on your website and other marketing materials.

Also use the award graphic in your booth at trade shows. Ask for permission to include a quote from the show or publication that gave the award, if one was written.

The Least You Need to Know

- ◆ Have at least one press announcement for every show.

- ◆ Start contacting media members the moment you hear about the first reporter who is attending.

- ◆ Your company or product by itself might not be considered newsworthy; spice things up with customer references or industry research you have done.

- ◆ Check out opportunities for best-of-show awards and participate when possible.

Chapter 12

Target Business Prospects

In This Chapter

- ◆ Understanding who your product is for
- ◆ Learn the differences between end users, customers, and decision makers and how good sales results are achieved by combining them
- ◆ Learn how to push decision makers' buttons
- ◆ Understanding the decision-making process so you can identify possible objections and obstacles
- ◆ Understanding and listing all the benefits of your solutions

Chapter 8 discussed the importance of really knowing your prospects so you can create effective and targeted messaging. This is just one area of trade show exhibiting where fully understanding your target prospects is a condition for success.

This chapter teaches you the information points to research and collect so you can gain a competitive edge, shorten sales cycles, and dramatically improve your return on investment (ROI) for your trade show exhibiting. Knowing your prospects' profile—such as their industry, business size, and job titles of purchasing decision makers—and how they use your product is what makes the trade show experience great. Many of the data points we need should be available within your company already, and any data gathered through your research should be shared with other departments because it is also key information for product management, sales, and marketing.

Business Profile Overview

Begin by creating a general overview of the types of businesses that currently use your products. Keep in mind that those businesses are not necessarily your sweet spot target customers. Those businesses might simply be your first group of customers because of existing sales channels or business relationships. To create a meaningful analysis, you have to create a list of all potential types of businesses that would be good customer candidates for your product. To gather this information, you have to work closely with several departments within your organization.

> **Show Smarts**
>
> If you have a product management department, check with it first. It should have comprehensive information on target customers. If it doesn't, see if you can get product management to do that work for you!

Ideal Business Size and Revenue

Start out by listing business sizes and their revenue ranges for each product you might showcase at trade shows. Update your report every time a new product is created or acquired. To make all this information a little more digestible, it is a good idea to use some predefined categories. Be aware, however, that a category such as "small business" may mean completely different things to different people. It doesn't matter how you define the categories, as long as each term means the same thing to everyone in your company.

In North America, for example, a "small business" is commonly defined as a company with 100 or fewer employees. I know many business owners who have maybe 60 employees and think of themselves as medium-size businesses or even enterprises. Of course, the number of employees is not the only way to categorize businesses; revenue is another popular method. However you decide to define the terms, make sure everyone is in sync about the meanings. If you currently have no definitions established in your company, use the following bullets as a guide:

♦ A small office/home office (SOHO) typically has 10 or fewer employees and is often operated from a home.

♦ A small business in North America typically is defined as a company with 11 to 100 employees.

♦ A medium-size business is a company with 101 to 500 employees.

♦ Large businesses are companies with more than 500 employees.

♦ Enterprises are often defined simply as Fortune 1000 companies.

♦ Public sector companies, from local municipalities to ministries, are not really businesses, but they should be treated as a category for your planning.

> **Show Smarts**
>
> Make sure everyone understands the definitions of the categories you use, especially if you work in a company with international offices. For example, the legal definition of "small business" in the European Union is 50 or fewer employees, while medium-size businesses have 51 to 250 employees.

Regional Location and Characteristics

As you know, there are significant differences in cultural behavior among geographical locations, whether you're comparing urban areas to rural, one state to another, or even two different countries. I live in Miami, Florida, and the pace of life and cultural behavior are fundamentally different in South Beach as compared to rural areas only 50 miles away. There are significant differences between urban and rural areas, and there are significant differences between states and countries, of course.

> **Don't Do It!**
>
> Never assume that a theme that works in one geographic area will work in another. For example, major metropolitan areas tend to be more liberal. Themes and messaging that work well in such an environment may not work at all in more conservative locations.

My point is that you need to know not only who your target prospects are but also where they are. This helps you fine-tune your messaging to their cultural needs as well as with the selection of regional trade shows. Depending on the geographic dispersion of your prospects, you may group them in a couple of categories. The results from this exercise are relevant to your trade show planning processes. They affect possible themes, colors, and many more items.

Industry Description and Associations

Your company may specialize in products for a specific industry such as finance or telecommunications. In marketing lingo, that is called a vertical focus. A good example of this is software for medical practices. This is a product aimed at a specific vertical, the health-care market. On the other side is the horizontal, which focuses on a specific need found horizontally across industries. A cell phone service is an example of a service that pretty much applies to any industry and hence has a horizontal marketing focus.

Consequently, if you have a product for a vertical market, you need to know your prospects' industries. Knowing the industries enables you to list industry associations, which in turn helps you find trade shows for your segments. Also your company may cater to subcategories. For example, trade shows are a subcategory of marketing and have their own industry associations.

Know Product Users and Prospects

To effectively sell and promote your products, you need to fully understand who your product users and prospects are. I am sure that you already have some description of who your users are, but in order to target them as effectively as possible, you have to know them inside out—what makes them tick, what their problems are, and what their daily work routine looks like.

For example, you should know exactly why they use your products, if they use them in conjunction with other products, and whether those products are your own or another company's. You should know what other products they considered and why they picked yours. It is not possible to know too much about your customers and prospects. The more information you can list the better. To facilitate the collection of all this data, create a file for each of your products.

Define Users and Customers for Each Product

Keep in mind that your customers and users may be different for each of your products. To understand how to position your company and your products, you have to realize that each product may have a different set of *users* as well as a different set of *customers*.

def•i•ni•tion

As related to the business-to-business (B2B) category: **users** are the individuals who use your products, and **customers** are the entities that buy your products.

How the Product Is Used

Now that you know who uses your product, explore how they use it. This includes how often it is used, for what purpose it is used, and whether it is used by a single user or a collaborative team.

Show Smarts

Never assume you know how your product is used. You'd be surprised by the unintended uses many products have. Make sure to research this fact. Often a quick e-mail survey does the trick.

List Your Product's Benefits

What benefits does your product provide for its users, its customers, and its decision makers? You need to list a couple benefits for each of the three categories, and you should find that there is little overlap.

Let's assume you make an accounting software package. Your customers might be medium-size businesses, your users are the people that work in their accounting departments, and the decision maker might be the CFO, because he decides on what accounting package to use. Let's list some possible benefits: The user may benefit because certain tasks have been simplified and now take less time. The company may benefit from reduced accounting costs, and the CFO may benefit from improved reporting. Each category has its own distinct benefits.

Characteristics of End Users and Customers

To effectively market your products, you also have to understand the characteristics of users and customers. Make a list of what defines your users. The list will be specific to your needs, but you should be able to answer the following questions about your end users:

- ◆ What are their work goals?
- ◆ What is important for them?
- ◆ Why would they care about your product?
- ◆ What are their pay grades, and how do they use your product?

You also need to understand the characteristics of your customers.

- ◆ Are they well funded or extremely budget conscious?
- ◆ What industry are they in?
- ◆ How do they buy products?
- ◆ Are there any regional differences or preferences?
- ◆ Are they all privately held or public companies?

The more you know about the characteristics of both the end users and customers, the better you can target your products.

 You'll find more information about the characteristics of end users and customers in Chapter 12 of the CD.

Why Current Customers Buy Your Product

There might be quite a few different reasons why current customers buy your products, and it's important to know those reasons. Price is often one of them, but specific features such as your warranty, service contracts, or the reputation of your company can be deciding factors. Sometimes customers are simply loyal to a specific reseller that happens to sell your product. Whatever the reasons might be, list them for each of your products and rank them in the order of importance to your customers. You might have to do a quick survey to get the answers you are looking for.

Reaching the Purchasing Decision Maker

Even if you have identified the ideal customer and its end users think your product is the best invention since sliced bread, this does not mean revenue for you unless you can reach the person, or group of persons, who makes purchasing decisions. Identifying the purchasing decision maker is crucial for your sales process.

There are two fundamentally different corporate philosophies. One is top to bottom, in which a senior manager makes a purchasing decision, and that decision then makes its way down the food chain. The other concept is bottom to top, in which low-level employees make purchasing recommendations that then work their way up to a decision maker, who largely follows the recommendations he or she receives. Of course, there are hybrids of both models, but in North America we lean toward the first, while in Asia the second approach is more prevalent. The main point here is that you need to understand who makes the purchasing decision and how to reach that person.

> **Show Smarts**
>
> Once you have identified decision makers, consider getting them VIP invitations or VIP show passes for the next trade show where you are an exhibitor.

Characteristics and Budget of the Decision Maker

Just as it is important to understand the characteristics of end users and customers, it is also important to understand the characteristics of decision makers. What makes them tick? What is important to them? Do they want to save as much money as possible, or do they want to buy the best possible tools? The more you know about the decision maker, the easier it is for your sales and marketing team to press the right buttons and achieve the desired results. Of course, pressing the right buttons is not effective unless your product fits into the company's budget.

It also helps to understand your prospect's budgeting process and what other budget items you are competing with. Let's revisit our previous accounting package example and assume it costs $35,000. If the customer's annual IT budget is $100,000, then our accounting package certainly fits in. However, the company also needs to upgrade the operating system on its desktop computers and the e-mail server, which is estimated to cost about $70,000. Now we are in competition with products that have nothing to do with our own. Knowing the various *pain points* of your customers enables you to position your product and its benefits in a way that your offering receives the necessary priority.

def•i•ni•tion

> **Pain points** are all the perceived problems and issues a prospect is facing

Product Pricing and Competitor Comparison

You also need to understand the product pricing of all your actual competitors. To stay with our example, these may be other companies that make accounting packages or possibly even companies providing accounting services. For each and every product you consider exhibiting at a trade show, you need to create a table that compares your offering and your product pricing with that of your competitors.

Show Smarts

While they don't necessarily have to be part of your comparison table, do consider indirect competitors. Indirect competitors are products that may solve a problem differently. To stay with our accounting package example, manual book keeping is an indirect competitor, though admittedly a rather weak one.

Product Offering, Service, and Benefits

There typically is more to a product offering than just price and features. Customers and decision makers evaluate a total offering, which includes items such as warranty, service levels, company reputation, popularity, and perceived reliability. All of these components are part of the benefits your product or solution provides, and all of these benefits are part of the purchasing process.

You have to realize there is more to a purchasing decision than basic functionality and price. If those two were the main factors, then companies like Hyundai would sell the most cars, and companies like Bentley wouldn't sell any. Coincidentally, this is a good example of two companies selling the same conceptual product, a car, in the same geographic market, yet they don't really compete.

Typical Product Purchasing Timeline

The last big item you have to research is typical purchasing timelines so you can accurately project how long it'll take your company to convert a lead into a customer. This is important to know because you want to determine your return on investment (ROI) on your trade show exhibiting activities.

For obvious reasons, if sales cycles are long, you won't know any accurate ROI information until those cycles are completed.

In order to reasonably estimate the sales cycles, you also have to understand the purchasing process of your prospects. This includes policies on product testing, competitive bids, and how an actual purchase is approved and who approves it.

Having this information allows you to focus on customers with a shorter purchasing timeline or to engage in marketing or public relations activities that help you shorten sales cycles.

Don't Do It!

Don't be overly optimistic about purchasing timelines. Remain conservative; otherwise, your ROI numbers in your postshow report will not look as good as they should.

Purchasing Obstacles to Overcome

Armed with all the information you collected, you and your sales team can now prepare to overcome the most common obstacles and objections that prevent you from closing a deal. It also allows you to focus on potential prospects where you expect less assistance. In any case, make a list of obstacles and objections and how to get around them.

The Least You Need to Know

◆ You need to know who your customers and end users are.

◆ The more you know about the characteristics of your end users, customers, and their decision makers, the easier it is to target the right companies and individuals.

◆ List the benefits for each of your products and compare your overall offering per product to that of your competitors.

◆ Learn your customer's decision-making and purchasing processes so you can take action to shorten sales cycles.

◆ Identify all obstacles and objections and figure out ways to overcome them.

Chapter 13

Lead Collection

In This Chapter

- The importance of gathering qualified leads rather than focusing on quantity
- Collaboration strategies for marketing and sales
- Distinguishing various lead-capturing options
- Creating a lead-collection, handling, and follow-up process
- Determining the best lead-qualifying questions to ask potential prospects

The most common reason why companies exhibit at trade shows is to collect sales leads. In its most basic form, a sales lead is contact information for an individual or an entity potentially interested in purchasing a product or service. But if all you needed to be successful was a large list of names and phone numbers, you wouldn't have to exhibit; you could simply buy the list of all attendees and be done with it. And if it was all that simple, I wouldn't have waited until now to tell you this.

Sales leads are what fuel your sales engine. Your sales organization depends on a continuous supply of leads, whether they are created through marketing campaigns, cold calling, or trade show exhibiting. Salespeople, like most of us humans, prefer the path of least resistance. If they have to choose between two lead sources, they will choose the one they believe will have the highest conversion rate.

Coming back with a large number of leads from a trade show might make you look good initially. However, that can change if your sales organization decides that contacting all of them to find the real prospects is too much hassle. In a worst-case scenario, sales starts ignoring your trade show leads completely, which as you can imagine will not help your ROI results. This makes it increasingly difficult to get funding for your trade show activities, brings you more scrutiny than you want, and, in the most extreme scenario, leaves you unemployed. None of these sounds like something you would want, so let's make sure you avoid them by producing qualified leads. This chapter walks you through processes necessary to do just that.

Qualified Leads

Good salespeople make a big impact on a sales organization, but anyone who can pick up a phone and select the right keys can close a deal if he or she has well-qualified leads. Leads can range from a contact who works in an industry that could use your product to a decision maker who already stated that he loves your product and would buy it right from the trade show floor if possible. The latter is a well-qualified lead.

There are, of course, many shades between these two examples, but it is easier to *convert* a well-qualified lead into a sale, and those conversions make the ROI numbers of your trade show. In the previous chapter, you created profiles of your ideal target prospects. As part of the materials for your booth staff training and the guide you provide them, you need to create a condensed "executive overview" version of that profile so that everyone can easily understand who you want as part of the lead-generation process.

def•i•ni•tion

Conversion, or lead conversion, is the process of converting an initial lead into a sale.

Remember Quality vs. Quantity

It is awfully tempting to want to bring back massive amounts of leads from a trade show. The number of leads is considered to be the first indication of the success of a show, how hard booth staff worked, and how well everything was planned, organized, and executed. As mentioned earlier, this will only look impressive until the sales team starts complaining about the quality of the leads and how it is unable to meet its quota trying to reach people that just stopped by your booth because they liked the free T-shirt or other promotional item you provided. If there is one area where the old phrase "quality versus quantity" applies, it is here. You will be much better off with a smaller number of leads that convert into sales than a large number of contacts your sales force is wasting time with. One of the huge advantages of trade show exhibiting is that you have direct contact and interaction with potential prospects, making it unusually easy to qualify and rank them.

Working With the Sales Organization

In most companies there is a silent, and in some cases a not-so-silent, animosity between the sales and marketing organizations. The sales group typically feels that the marketing department doesn't provide it with all the tools and leads it needs to be successful, while the marketing department thinks that the sales organization is making poor use of the material already provided.

There is typically some truth to both sides of the story, but this starts to matter less when you realize that sales is really marketing's "customer." Once marketing realizes this and treats sales accordingly, it is easier to agree on common goals. It motivates the marketing organization to better understand the sales process, the sales organization's responsibilities, and how they are compensated. Understanding this can be a big eye opener for marketing professionals and can change the relationship between the two departments.

Lead-Qualifying Questions

You have already determined your target prospects. Hopefully, your booth design, messaging, and surrounding marketing activities attract the right audience. But because people don't walk around with little stickers on their foreheads describing their lead type, you need to ask some qualifying questions. The more you know about an attendee, the easier it is for sales to decide what to do with the lead.

To do this, you need to plan an organized approach that involves defining a set of qualifying questions. These questions should enable you to categorize, rank, and qualify attendees as efficiently as possible. Booth staffers should listen for and note any additional information a prospect volunteers about his needs. This helps sales with the follow-up process. Ranking prospects helps you with your postshow report while the leads are still in the sales cycle and enables you to track your daily show performance toward reaching your trade show goals.

Review Key Prospects

Asking the sales department what kind of information is most helpful to it in closing a prospect is a good basis for creating your qualifying questions. Correlate that with your key prospects' profiles and you are well on your way to identifying the most important questions to ask.

Formulating Your Qualifying Questions

Make a list of the top 5 to 10 things that the sales team stated are the most important to know. If you have an experienced sales force, you have almost all of the ingredients needed to create your qualifying questions. The information your salespeople need varies, but will typically include the expected purchase timeframe, what solution the prospect is currently using, the size of the company, and what budget there is for a new solution.

Since the primary purpose of these questions is to rate and rank leads, your questions should have multiple-choice answers, greatly simplifying that process. You don't want to lose the attendees' attention and their willingness to answer your questions. The questions should be easy to answer and limited to no more than three or four qualifying questions. As part of this process, you will also indirectly get answers to other qualifying questions such as job title, which reveals the decision-making power of the individual, or the company address, which tells you what region they are from.

Show Smarts _____

Sometimes the lead scan system provided by the show gives you access to registration data that the prospect supplied when signing up for the show. This often includes information such as company size and industry. If this information is provided, don't waste valuable time by asking questions already answered through this system.

Lead Capture Methods

Now that you have a good idea as to what information you want to capture, you need to look at the available methods and technologies that achieve this. Before you decide on an approach, find out what *customer relationship management* (*CRM*) solution your sales force uses. Frequently, there are optional software solutions that enable you to upload data from your lead-capturing system directly into the CRM system your company uses.

def•i•ni•tion _____

Customer relationship management (CRM) is the processes implemented by a business to handle all of its contacts with customers and prospects. In most cases, a software solution supports these processes by storing customer and prospect information and applying logic to this data to facilitate sales follow-up, trigger marketing campaigns, and help with reporting.

Paper-Based Lead Forms

Paper-based lead forms are certainly the most inexpensive method for collecting lead information, but manually typing the results into a data-processing system back in the office can cost you those savings. However, lead forms do have a couple of advantages. The most prominent one is the ability to easily write notes on them; the second most important one is that paper-based lead forms scale well.

Unlike electronic lead-capturing methods, you can pretty much hand out as many lead forms as needed at any given point in time. Even if you decide against paper-based forms as your primary lead-capturing method, I recommend always having some lead forms available in case your booth gets too busy or you experience technical difficulties with your other lead-capturing system.

Show Smarts _____

Each lead form needs to have space for contact information. To simplify this, have staplers available so that prospects or booth staffers can staple business cards to the forms. Also, make sure you have an ample supply of pens. Even if you use the cheapest pens around, attendees will walk off with them. I have never quite figured out why!

Lead Capture Rental from the Show

Almost every show offers this option but usually provides limited flexibility in customizing it for questions. Some of the systems do provide additional information that the show organizer captured about the attendee, such as job title, industry, and company size.

Before you make any decision, make sure you understand exactly what kind of data is captured and provided and what options you have to add customized questions. Remember that your mission is to provide qualified leads, and if the show-provided capture system does not supply you with the ability to do that, it is not really an option.

Custom Lead Capture Systems

There are many good solutions on the market, and most support the common bar codes or magnetic cards used by most shows. Prices vary greatly by manufacturer and included features, and almost all of them allow for customized qualifying questions. What makes custom lead-capturing systems valuable is their ability to interface directly with the most popular CRM system. This enables you to start the lead follow-up process within minutes of capturing a lead. For example, you can often e-mail data sheets or assign the lead to a salesperson while the attendee is still in the booth.

Hybrids

Just like hybrid cars are increasingly popular because they combine gas engines with electric propulsion, in the trade show industry, a hybrid lead machine is one that combines paper forms with a custom lead-capturing system, giving you the best of both worlds. I try to avoid promoting any particular product in this book, but the CardScan® Lead Qualifier is a product I feel compelled to mention.

This solution uses customized and preprinted paper-based forms that can then be scanned and uploaded to a CRM system. Business cards are affixed to a sticky area on the form, which also has a place for written notes. When scanned, the notes are saved as a graphic, and the salesperson can read the notes in the CRM system.

Don't Do It!

CardScan Lead Qualifier is a proprietary product designed to work with specific hardware. You can't use its forms with the company's traditional CardScan business card reader systems or any other scanner or software.

Setting a Plan Before the Show

When you define the questions for your lead-gathering process, you also need to define what happens to the leads once you have them. Don't wait until after the show to decide how to attack your collected leads; your competition may have already contacted your prospects by then. Good preshow planning of lead handling and processing improves your odds of converting the leads into sales. Working with the sales team creates a smooth process and ensures that everyone "buys in" to the process.

 You can find more information on lead fulfillment planning in Chapter 13 of the CD.

Responsible Parties and Tasks

There are lead-planning and follow-up tasks that have to be completed before and after the show. If you have the authority to assign them yourself, great! Otherwise, make sure to start early with the respective managers to avoid any holes in the process.

The following is a list of tasks that have to be planned and assigned:

- ◆ Define a written lead-collection process and update with data as the tasks are completed and decisions have been made regarding the items in this list.

- ◆ Assign a code for each trade show so that you can track leads easier.

- ◆ Create the lead-qualifying questions and select a lead capture method.

- ◆ Enter the lead questions into the capture system and CRM as required.

- ◆ Design and order paper lead forms.

- ◆ Define the lead-scoring process.

- ◆ Define the booth staff procedures for collecting and handling leads.

- ◆ Define the lead follow-up process once leads reach the office.

- ◆ Create follow-up materials before the show.

Show Smarts

As always, you may need to customize this checklist to meet your specific needs. Depending on your organization's experience with exhibiting and lead processing, more or less detail might be needed. For example, you may want to spell out who in the office receives the leads and how quickly they have to be entered into the CRM system. On the other hand, if those processes are already well defined and implemented, they don't have to be listed.

Lead Follow-Up Process and Materials

The lead follow-up process is key to converting leads into customers. It has to be defined and worked out with the sales department well in advance. For example, you want to create follow-up e-mails specific to groups of attendees and the products that interested them. You may also decide that a snail mail follow-up process is warranted, with letters signed by specific salespeople.

In many cases, you define variances of lead follow-up processes based on the lead's score. An immediate follow-up phone call is justified, with much personal attention, for some leads. For others, an automated follow-up e-mail is all that is warranted. This is why lead scoring and a defined lead follow-up process based on score are so important; they facilitate the best use of corporate resources. It is also important that each item or process has an assigned deadline.

Informing Booth Staff of Procedures

Your booth staff training must emphasize the importance of following all procedures regarding lead collection, handling, and scoring. We covered this in Chapter 9, but mistakes made on the show floor when handling leads are next to impossible to correct. Make sure everyone fully understands the process and what to do with leads.

Lead Scoring Procedure

As previously discussed, you want to help sales as much as possible in converting leads to customers—not only because it is more pleasant to work with happy salespeople, but also because the success of your show results depends on it. The best way to make sure that sales focuses on the right leads in the right order is to score the leads and categorize them. Do this in as close to real time as possible, at least daily during the show.

It is important to have defined ahead of time how and when the scoring is to be done and what it means to the sales organization. You may have categories such as 1 through 5, A through F, or whatever schema you have come up with to rank your leads. It really isn't very important what ranking schema you choose. What is important is that everyone involved fully understands how it works and what it means. Unless you have an automated system that scores the leads based on the multiple-choice answers, paper-based leads have to be scored before they are processed. In most cases, writing the score on the paper form works best. This can be done by each booth staffer or by dedicated personnel at the end of the day. If you capture the leads electronically, scoring should happen at the time the lead is captured. If the attendee can see the screen of the capturing device, make sure the scoring code is not too obvious or rude.

Lead Process At-Show

The process you choose to get leads back to the office and your sales force depends on your lead capture method and your technical capabilities to process leads quickly. In most cases, you want your leads in the hands of your sales force as quickly as possible. If you are using paperbased forms, using an overnight courier is a popular option. If they are in electronic format, you might be able to e-mail them or upload them directly to your CRM system.

Show Smarts

If you decide to send paper leads daily, make photo copies before sending them in case the shipping service loses them.

The Least You Need to Know

- Sales and marketing need to collaborate to create a plan that best uses existing resources to follow up on leads.

- Put a strong emphasis on getting high-quality leads rather than a high quantity of leads.

- Always ask prospects qualifying questions that enable you to score the lead so it can be prioritized for follow-up.

- Assign tasks and responsibilities for each part of the lead-management process well before the show starts.

- Prepare follow-up material and have it ready to go when the leads come in.

- Make sure each booth staffer understands how the leads will be processed and what his or her responsibilities are in that process.

Chapter 14

Thoroughly Know Your Competitors

In This Chapter

- ◆ Learn the importance of understanding your competitive landscape
- ◆ Use research about your competitors to decide where and how to exhibit
- ◆ Differentiate yourself and your products from your competition
- ◆ Learn where to find competitor information

A wise person once said, "Keep your friends close and your enemies closer." This is not to say that all competitors are enemies; as a matter of fact, a surprisingly large number of companies benefit from having competitors. Consequently, understanding the competitive forces in your industry and what they mean for your exhibiting is important enough to dedicate a chapter to it. Why? Because when you exhibit at a trade show, you want to stand out. This means you have to differentiate yourself, and you can only do that if you know your competitors.

Reasons to Track Trade Show Competitors

In addition to needing to know how to differentiate yourself, there are a couple other reasons to track your competitors' exhibiting activities. There are times when you want to avoid going head-to-head with certain competitors, and there are times when you don't want to miss a show where a certain competitor is exhibiting. It is always helpful to know exactly where your competitors are and where they are heading.

Types of Competitors

When you look at competitors, don't just look at companies that offer a similar—or even identical—products to yours.

There are also other competing influences that may affect a prospect's decision to buy your product. To illustrate this point, I am going to use a car manufacturer as an example. To track competitors for your business, make a list of all companies or solutions from the following three categories that you perceive to be a threat to your market position. Also keep in mind that competitors change, so update your list every once in a while.

Direct Competitors

There are, of course, direct competitors. For our example, those would be other car makers that have a vehicle with similar features aimed at the same potential customer.

Indirect Competitors

In addition to direct competitors, there are companies that offer alternative solutions to the prospect's problem. In our example, a family needs to buy a second car to commute to work. Several car makers compete for that business, but there are also other solutions to the family's problem. Competing solutions in this case might include public transit, a motor bike maker, or a town car service. Moving closer to work might even be a solution. Those would be indirect competitors.

Future Competitors

Future competitors are companies or solutions that invade your space sometime down the road. In our car example, that might include foreign car makers that don't currently offer their products here but will enter the local market at some point. This would be a future direct competitor. Advances in communication technology may lead to a large number of people working from home, making commuting to work obsolete in the future. So you see, something seemingly unrelated to a car manufacturer, such as the Internet, may become an indirect competitor in the future.

Where to Find Your Competitors

Odds are, you already know the majority of your competitors. Nobody knows better who your competitors are than a good sample of your customers. But there are also other ways to find out who your competitors are. The following list provides an easy means to find them. Use the competitor analysis spreadsheet to create a list of competitors with their relevant company and product information.

- ◆ **Search engines:** Enter keywords related to your company and products.

- ◆ **Industry publications:** Look within the articles and the advertisements.

- ◆ **Trade shows:** Attend industry trade shows to see what competition is in the market. Look at the exhibitors and ask around at the networking events.

- ◆ **Trade show websites:** Research industry trade shows to see what companies are exhibiting, read their company descriptions, and find their websites.

- ◆ **Your sales department:** It should know who or what it lost business to.

 You can find a competitor analysis spreadsheet in Chapter 14 of the CD.

> **Don't Do It!**
>
> Before you spend a lot of time collecting competitor information, first ask other departments such as sales, marketing, and product management if they already have a competitive analysis report.
>
> If they don't, consider hiring a firm to create one for you. Don't tie up your business's internal resources if you don't have to. Get a few quotes to find out how much these services cost, and then make an informed decision on whether your budget (or possibly the combined budgets from marketing, sales, and product management) can pay for these services. It can be an eye opener to get an outsider's view of your competitive landscape. If hiring a firm doesn't fit the budget, try to divide up the work to create a competitive analysis among the various departments.

Where to Find Competitor Information

Once you have made a list of competitors to track, you need to find out more information about them. There are many sources that can provide you with different perspectives on the activities and positions of your competitors.

The following table outlines some of the places you can look for information. Keep in mind that not all of these will be relevant for finding information on your competitors. You need to determine the most targeted places to search.

Places to Find Competitor Information

Company website	Online networking portals
Press releases	Search engines
Trade shows	Industry analysts
Conferences	Suppliers
Panel sessions	Partners
Reps and distributors	Networking

Competitor Websites

The first place to check out a competitor's information is its website. While information about its products and the company should be available, keep in mind that the site has been created by marketing folks who aim to present their products and company the way they want them to be perceived, which is not necessarily what they actually are.

Show Smarts

If the competitor has a customer service section on the website that enables customers to ask and answer questions publicly, check that area carefully. It may offer you a glimpse into what the company's real strengths and weaknesses are. Use this as a competitive advantage for your marketing and trade show approaches.

Networking Events, Seminars, and Trade Shows

Networking events, seminars, and trade shows offer a different perspective of your competitors. At networking events, you can chat with people who use their products or with business partners who sell their solutions. Often those people share a fair amount of information.

Trade shows enable you to see competitors' products or possibly even try them out. And of course, if you see them at a trade show, you can learn a lot about their exhibiting strategy and execution. In Chapter 17 you will learn more about collecting competitor information at trade shows.

Online

The Internet is a tool that can provide a constant flow of competitive information. Besides websites of user groups, blogs, and media publications, search engine tools provide you with powerful options to keep tabs on your competitors' exhibiting activities.

Show Smarts

Of all the online alert services, Google Alerts is my favorite for easily tracking competitor activities. It enables you to create search terms such as "[competitor name] show." Google then sends you an e-mail every day it finds a new match for your search term. It is a free service with no limit to the number of search terms you can create.

If you elect to receive a large number of alerts, you may want to consider routing them to a special e-mail folder.

Your Sales Team

Another good source for competitive information is your own sales group because it is constantly facing prospects who have to decide among competing solutions. Ask what made customers choose your company if you won business and why you lost it if you didn't win the business.

Compile Facts and Materials About Competitors

Many areas contribute to the complete picture of what your competitors are up to. The more information you have, the more complete that picture will be and the more accurately you can exploit your competitors' weaknesses and position your business for success.

In Chapter 14 of the CD, you will find a sample spreadsheet to help you to track information about your competitors. Customize it to fit your business's needs. Currently, there are only two rows listed for competitors. Add as many rows as you need for all the competitors you identify and research. This helps your company gain advantages not only at trade shows but also in product management, branding, and general marketing.

Company Details: Strengths, Weaknesses, Sales Team

Know what each competitor's strengths and weaknesses are. Find out the size of its sales team and how it is organized. Know if the company sells directly or through resellers and, if so, who and where those resellers are.

Product Offerings and Pricing

Research your competitors' product offerings and how those products or services are priced. Often there is a huge difference between list price and the actual sales price, so make sure to have both of those data points if there is a marked difference between them.

Their Customers

Know who your competitors' customers are. Companies that have a similar product often have established a niche and focus only on specific industries. Knowing what those are helps you decide if there are trade show audiences you want to avoid or what shows to exhibit at if you decide to attack a competitor's position.

Media Coverage, Marketing Materials, and Advertisements

Track your competitors' media coverage and advertisements. Knowing what media they use and which publications they have little or no coverage in can help your trade show marketing plan.

Complete Exhibit List and Booth Sizes

Make a list of all the trade shows each competitor has exhibited at during the previous year and the shows the competitor is confirmed for or expected to be exhibiting at this year. Note the booth size used at each show. A few companies list their complete trade show schedules on their websites, but in most cases you have to keep updating this as information becomes available. Make sure to differentiate between confirmed shows and suspected shows.

Competitor Trade Show Marketing Approaches

List the marketing approaches your competitors take with their trade shows:

- What shows do they sponsor activities at in addition to exhibiting?
- Do they use preshow mailers or e-mails?
- What publications do they advertise in preshow?
- Do they advertise in the show guide?
- Do they use show hall ads or billboards on the show floor or outside?
- Do they offer live presentations in their booths?

Competitor Public Relations Approaches

Because public relations is an important part of your trade show activities, you also have to understand your competitors' approaches to PR. Short of violating the wire tapping act, this is a little bit more difficult to research.

Of course, you can track competitors' press releases and press conferences. But figuring out what publications they target and how they position themselves to various media contacts is much harder. Getting a press kit from the press room at a show may help you understand their positioning, but what media they go after can only be guessed from the results of their efforts.

Show Smarts

When tracking competitor press releases, you should track all general press releases as well as trade show press releases. A sample template is provided for you to track the number of releases distributed by your top 10 competitors each month. Additionally, track the number of press mentions they receive per month.

Tracking this information helps you evaluate how your company's public relations initiatives compare to competitors and whether you need to focus on increasing your business's activities to gain a competitive advantage. If you have the budget, consider subscribing to a press clipping service to track your main competitors.

Competitor-Sponsored Special Events

Research what special events your competitors sponsor and detail the audience that those events target. If you gain attendance, write a description of the event including what occurred and what the turnout was.

Network with attendees to casually gain information about the competitor. Always write notes about conversations while they are fresh in your memory so you can reference them as needed.

Using the Data to Your Advantage

Of course I didn't have you collect and compile all this data to simply use up space on your computer's hard drive. Analyzing this data enables you to make smarter decisions for your own trade show activities, plans, and goals.

Your individual situation and goals determine how you use the information you collected, whether you want to outperform a specific competitor or you want to avoid direct competition.

Your Show Selections and Booth Sizes

The big question here is whether you want to take on a competitor directly. Either way, knowing the shows and booth sizes of your competitors enables you to select the best combinations to meet your own goals.

If your targeted competitors are not exhibiting at the same shows you selected, use the list of the competitors' shows as a guide for selecting next year's shows.

Products You Bring to the Shows

Another key question your competitive information helps answer is what products to bring and showcase when you exhibit. Again, your choice depends on how directly you choose to compete.

Conveying Your Product's Competitive Advantages

Whether you decide to compete directly or not, understanding your competitors' product positions and their strengths and weaknesses enables you to position your products and trade show messaging in a way that differentiates you from your competitors.

It is important that your prospects understand that your products are different. Otherwise, the only decision point prospects have to select your product is over your competitors' price. This is a situation you want to avoid.

Marketing, Public Relations, and Event Planning

Knowing your competitors' preshow activities, events, and PR strategy allows you to make the decision either to stay out of each other's way or to compete directly.

Consider this event-planning question. If a fairly equal competitor holds an event for attendees, should your company budget to hold an event as well and try to upstage it? This is a tough decision. If the event and attendance are a hit, prospects see you as a solid competitor. But if the event is a flop, your competitors find you to be weak and use this to their advantage.

Using Data for Business Advantages

Your ability to differentiate yourself based on competitive information is key to all aspects of your business, not just trade shows. It may affect what information you share on your website, how you develop your PR, and your event strategy. It even affects the roadmap of your products. The most important part to understand is that no two companies can have the same image in a prospect's mind. To successfully beat your competition, you have to be perceived differently.

Sometimes you can even take a negative and use it to your advantage. Many of you may remember the Avis car rental campaign in which Avis admitted that it was not the market leader. Its "We're not number one, but we try harder" campaign helped to create the image of being similar to the market leader but to expect higher service and more customer attention because it had to put more effort into catching up.

The Least You Need to Know

- ◆ You need to understand your competitive landscape in order to plan your own marketing and trade show activities.

- ◆ Use tools like Google Alerts to stay informed without much effort.

- ◆ Competitive information is key to deciding whether you want to compete directly or avoid shows with specific competitors.

- ◆ To succeed, you have to differentiate yourself from your competitors in the prospect's mind.

Part 4

Final Prep and Showtime!

You are racing to the finish line. Now you have to figure out the remaining logistical items such as getting your booth to the show location, setting it up, and creating a contingency plan in case you need one.

Once you arrive in the show city, don't expect to have a free minute. After you check into your hotel, it's time to go to the event venue, get your exhibitor passes, and get your booth set up and tested. During the show, expect to deal with minor emergencies and to constantly work with your booth staff to stay on track toward reaching your goals. The show time will pass quickly, and once the breakdown begins, you will have to avoid a couple of costly traps before you can make your way to the airport.

Chapter 15

Shipping Crates and Material Handling

In This Chapter

◆ Getting your display and booth material safely to the show

◆ Selecting the right shipping company for your needs

◆ Packing your material for shipment

◆ Considering different freight options

◆ Insuring your goods and what to do if they don't arrive

Getting your display safely to and from the show can be a major undertaking, depending on the size, weight, and materials you are shipping. If your booth is small enough to be transported by regular services such as FedEx ground, you probably won't have to worry too much about the information in this chapter. If a race car is part of your display or if you have to ship a large number of fragile items or items that are sensitive to temperatures, then welcome to the science of shipping and packaging. The information in this chapter is specific to domestic shipping. Shipping across borders adds a whole new level of complexity that is covered in Chapter 21 about international exhibiting.

Selecting a Shipping Company

There are several types of shipping companies, each with its own unique set of offerings and specialties. Selecting the right company depends a lot on what you are shipping to the show and how much time you have to get it there. You may choose to do the legwork yourself and request quotes from various shipping companies, or you may opt to use a freight broker. Once you explain what you are shipping and what your requirements are, the broker does the work necessary to get the best price for you.

To put this in perspective, selecting the type of shipping company or freight broker to work with is similar to picking an insurance company. You can choose to go directly to a specific insurance company, or you can use an insurance broker who tries to find the best policy based on your requirements. Also similar to the insurance example, the better you know what you want or need and the more you understand your options, the less need you have for a broker.

Types of Shipping Companies

There are several different types of shipping companies. As you might imagine, not every shipping company fits into one of these categories, but the following list is a good start toward understanding the different types of options.

♦ **Common carriers** are often one of the least expensive options, but transportation times often depend on how long it takes to get enough customers to fill a truck heading to a certain destination. You should expect longer transit times on equipment that is often not *air-ride* equipped.

♦ **Freight forwarders** are companies that often operate their own trucks but also broker shipments to partner carriers. Because of this additional flexibility, they can typically provide both air and ground service. More often than not, these services are competitively priced, and air-ride equipment is usually provided for ground transportation. Since freight forwarders often offer multiple shipping types, these companies can usually meet a number of different needs.

- A **van line** is an air-ride service, sometimes referred to as "white glove" service since these companies usually provide many additional services that regular carriers do not. This includes services such as pad-wrapping of freight. Prices tend to be higher, and often van lines do not unload freight, requiring third-party unloading labor for that process.

- **Show carriers** are not really a category themselves; they fit into one of the categories previously mentioned. Most frequently they are freight forwarders. I mention them here because they often provide show-specific services and discounts.

def•i•ni•tion

Air ride refers to the shock system found in the trailers. Like shocks in a car, air ride provides a smoother ride for your freight. The less your shipment gets bumped around, the lower the odds of something breaking.

Customer Service Options

Being able to reach someone who can help you when something goes wrong with your shipment is invaluable when it comes to dealing with issues under a strict deadline. No matter what type of company you choose, it should provide you with 24/7 customer service. It doesn't matter if that means a big call center or someone sleeping by a phone, as long as that person is empowered to help you when you need it.

The availability of a personal customer service assistant is nice to have but is not required. However, these people know you, your requirements, and what shows you attend, which can abbreviate many customer service calls because you won't have to tell your life story over and over again. Several shipping companies also provide show schedule management. You can get one quote for all your trade shows, including all your special requirements, which can be very useful if you are participating in a show tour that moves from city to city. In that case, the company should be able to assist with everything from paperwork to serving as liaisons between the van operator, the *drayage company*, and the exhibiting customer.

def•i•ni•tion

A **drayage company** is essentially the material handling company at the show site. Originally the term meant "to transport with a sideless cart," but today it primarily describes the company that manages all goods and freight entering and leaving a trade show.

Shipment Tracking Options

Selecting a vendor that provides online tracking of shipments, similar to the ability to track a package being sent via UPS or FedEx, not only gives you extra peace of mind but also instant access to your shipment's location without having to call customer services. Typically, if a company offers online tracking, the trucks have a GPS tracker installed so that you can locate your freight wherever it is in real time.

To facilitate all this, your freight items are usually labeled with a bar code upon pickup, and your paperwork receives a sticker with the same bar code or codes. Those codes are then scanned and electronically inventoried at loading, similar to baggage handling at airports. To track your shipments online, you are usually given access to a secure website with your own username and password. If web-based access is not provided, other options include the ability to call customer service, which has access to tracking tools or can even contact the driver directly.

Show Smarts

Always have an emergency number for customer service that you can reach 24/7. When problems arise close to the show dates and times, ask for the driver's cell phone number so you can communicate with him directly and expedite the process.

Company Experience, History, and Capabilities

Getting your display and material to the show on time is crucial. One of the worst things that can happen at a trade show is having no booth or blowing your budget by having to rent one at the last minute, reprint graphics, and purchase supplies related to the display and booth.

Your shipping company's performance is too important to risk it all just to save a couple dollars using "fly-by-night" companies and startups that don't have a history in the industry. I strongly recommend checking with the top trade show associations such as Exhibit Designers and Producers Association (EDPA), Exhibitor Appointed Contractor Association (EACA), Trade Show Exhibitors Association (TSEA), and Healthcare Convention and Exhibitors Association (HCEA) to make sure the company is a supporting member. Ask for references!

To a certain degree, you should treat the selection of a shipping company almost like a job interview for a new employee. The following are questions to help you judge and rank possible contenders:

◆ How many shows do you ship to per year?

◆ What percentage of your business is trade show/event related?

◆ Are you familiar with the particular convention center where we are exhibiting?

◆ Do you have a representative on-site?

◆ What companies do you work with that have needs similar to our own?

◆ Do you have an escalation process if there is a problem and customer service seems unable to help?

Pricing Considerations

Don't pay for what you don't need! Spending more money does not necessarily mean better service or more service. Know your requirements so that you only order and pay for the particular services your delivery requires. When shopping for quotes, be wary of companies that try to lead you away from your actual needs. If your shipment is not fragile, consider a common carrier unless you need the extra services provided by a van line. As with anything in business, shop the rates a bit and compare the offers. Watch out for extra charges, but realize that some of these are unavoidable such as paperwork preparation fees or waiting time.

Shipping Cases, Labeling, and Packing

As with choosing a shipping company, you need to know your needs before you decide on shipping cases and packaging. There are enough options out there to dedicate a book just to this topic. Anything exists in any size and any material, with and without foam, with and without handles, and with and without little pouches for accompanying paperwork. Later in this section we cover labeling and packing for each show to optimize space usage and to make sure your items get there on time.

Shipping Case Options

Shipping cases are made by a variety of manufacturers with wide ranges in price, quality, sizes, and options. Almost every manufacturer sells through a large network of distributors, so you should be able to find a local one and look at the products in person rather than rely on a marketing description in a catalog or on a website.

- **Cardboard boxes:** Nothing is cheaper than a cardboard box, which, if necessary, can be acquired for free by visiting the dumpster of the closest shopping mall. A cardboard box with plenty of tape around it is a great option for anything that does not need a sturdy, protective case. Cardboard boxes are also low in weight, further keeping costs down.

- **Plastic cases:** Designed to hold signs and other large, flat items, these cases are made from sturdy plastic and come in a variety of sizes to fit your displays. They are fairly thin, usually only about 6" to 10", and they may come with wheels for easier transportation.

- **Shipping crates:** Made of either wood or plastic, these specialized containers are sturdy and designed for a variety of shipping needs. They usually stack well together, making them a good option for larger items or a collection of smaller items that end up in storage.

Specialized containers exist for all standard items you could possibly need at a trade show. If you have a custom-made display, it often comes with a custom-made—or at least custom-modified—shipping container.

The majority of specialized cases are designed to make it possible to transport displays yourself. You should try to avoid dragging things around whenever possible, but if you do have to take matters into your own hands, pick from one of the many plastic containers with straps and wheels.

Best Practices for Packing Your Shipment

Some of the items mentioned here may seem extremely obvious. But when you are in the middle of managing all the aspects of a trade show, it's easy to miss even obvious things. I strongly suggest creating a list of best practices specific to your company. The following are tips to get you going:

◆ Always have a checklist for the contents of each case or box you ship. Place copies of those checklists inside the container so that when your booth staff or labor packs up at the end of the show, there is no confusion about what goes where.

◆ Number or name each of your boxes or cases and mark that name on the checklist.

◆ Always pack heavy items on the bottom, lighter ones on top.

◆ Avoid packing unnecessary items. Remember that you are charged for weight, and anything you ship that you don't need adds weight to your shipment as well as your budget.

◆ Wrap fragile items well and mark the box itself as fragile. Let the shipping company know you have fragile items and what they are.

Show Smarts

Place extra copies of the content checklists for each of your shipping containers in your master planning binder. That way you always have one available when it is time to pack up.

Labeling

Each time you send a shipment, be sure to remove shipping labels from previous shipments to avoid confusion and a possible cross-country trip for your box. Label each case clearly, either by copying the labels provided by the show in the exhibitor kit and taping them onto the case or by printing them on label paper. Another possible option is to use labels provided by your shipping carrier.

If you use labels provided by the show, make sure you select the proper label. There is often one type for shipping directly to the show and another one for shipping to the advance warehouse. The benefit of using show-provided labels is that you only need to fill in a few simple items such as where the case comes from, the exhibiting company, the booth number, the shipping carrier, and the number of pieces in the total shipment. Everything else is already preprinted with the correct information.

Shipping Planning Tasks

It is always a good idea to plan your shipping tasks well in advance. I recommend creating a task list that becomes part of your show binder. Make any such task list specific to your company's needs. The following ideas are just meant to give you a head start:

◆ Pack your shipment and add any supplies that need replenishing as well as items newly added to the exhibit. Make sure to update your checklists.

◆ If you outsource the assembly of your display, inform your display house of the show so it can manage those tasks for you.

◆ Arrange shipment for the upcoming show or shows. Describe what you intend to ship and any specific needs you have.

◆ Know the weight of the shipment and the size of the cases; the shipping company needs this information to determine what type of truck is best suited for your needs.

◆ Inform the shipping company of freight check-in times for both the beginning of the show—if shipping directly to the show site—and the close of the show.

◆ Get written confirmation from your shipping company of your order, including the expected pickup dates and times. Have the company confirm the show check-in times in writing.

- Track the progress of your shipment online or call the shipping company if needed.

- Always fill in the material handling forms. Preprint them if possible.

- Fill in and submit a form called the "preprinted outbound material handling request." That way, you can pick up your material handling form already preprinted on the last day of the show.

Saving Money

Your goal is to have your items arrive at the right place at the right time and in the same condition you shipped them. You should try to save as much money as you can while still achieving just that. The following are some money-saving tips:

- Always know the weight of your shipment so that you can verify the bill.

- If your display components have been wrapped in a moving pad, consider shipping your display components on a pallet. This saves on shipping and material handling (drayage) costs and reduces the risk of damage.

- Items on pallets can be received at the advance warehouse, whereas loose items typically can't be received there.

- Consolidate your exhibit, collateral, and supplies into one shipment to reduce drayage charges and eliminate minimum charges.

- You can often carry smaller booths on the plane, which eliminates shipping costs altogether. But be aware that airlines are increasingly charging for extra bags.

- Ship your freight straight to the show site instead of the general contractor's warehouse. Do this by instructing your carrier to deliver on the first "direct to show site" date and at the earliest possible time.

- Avoid forced freight. Chapter 18 describes this in more detail.

Show Smarts _____

If you decide to take your booth items with you on the plane and you have one or more frequent fliers on your staff, have them check in the bags. Airlines often waive extra bag charges for their best customers.

Categories of Freight

To provide the level of service each exhibitor needs, shipping companies came up with a number of different freight categories. Because every shipment won't fit neatly into a category, you have many available options. The shipping company makes arrangements for the most appropriate way to move your shipment to the show site, depending on your needs. Sample needs might include the size of the shipment, temperature-sensitive shipments, and the need to move heavy equipment. This section describes several freight categories in more detail to help you express your needs better when you arrange shipping to each show and to help you better understand some of the available options.

Full Truckload

Full truckload carriers fill a trailer with freight going to one single destination. The driver then proceeds directly to the *consignee* and usually delivers the freight himself. The biggest advantage of full truckload shipping is that there usually is no handling during transport whatsoever. The trailer arrives just as it left its origin.

def•i•ni•tion_____

Consignee is the shipping term for the person or entity receiving a shipment.

Less Than Full Truckload

Shipments too small to justify a dedicated trailer typically weigh between 100 and 10,000 lbs. Less-than-truckload carriers pick up freight from several different customers. All of the collected freight is placed onto trailers and then brought to a facility that sorts the shipments for yet additional transport.

Expedited

If you are in a rush, expedited shipping usually means your shipment arrives by air freight. Naturally, your shipment is picked up and delivered by a truck but is then loaded onto an aircraft for the majority of the distance. Air freight is booked through specialized air freight carriers or through a freight broker.

Always keep in mind that expedited freight is costly; try to avoid situations that require expedited freight unless it is absolutely necessary.

> **Budget Savers**
>
> Expedited shipping is expensive. Often two to three days additional notice makes the difference between a truck and air freight. Plan your shipping early for significant savings.

Refrigerated/Heated

If your freight needs to be temperature controlled, then you need to look for a transporter that has either heated or refrigerated trucks, depending on your needs. Specialized trucks keep your products at the temperature required. Shipping temperature-intolerant items to a trade show is rare. But after years in the industry, I have seen it all.

Flatbed

A flatbed truck is exactly what it sounds like. These trucks are typically used for very large equipment that does not fit into a traditional truck with sides and a roof.

Know the Weight of Your Shipment

When you shop around for quotes or just check your bill, you need to know the weight of your shipment. The weight of your shipment is the higher of either the actual weight or dimensional weight, often referred to as dim weight. The following are the common formulas used to determine dimensional weight.

Domestically

The domestic dim factor is 175. So you calculate length times width times height and divide it by the dim factor of 175.

Internationally

The international dim factor is 166. So you calculate length times width times height and divide it by the dim factor of 166.

Freight Insurance

The law requires carriers to provide liability insurance, which is usually 10 cents per pound. So unless you ship popcorn, this won't cover your cost in the case of a loss. To insure your shipment for its actual value, you have to get supplementary freight insurance that comes at an extra cost.

If Your Shipment Doesn't Arrive

Insured or not insured, the display not arriving is at the top of nightmare scenarios for trade show managers. While I have seen people sitting on an empty floor space with a hand-written sign saying, "XYZ carrier lost my booth. Ask me about ABC products," this is not the preferred solution. A better option is to inquire with show services about renting a display. You can arrange for printing of the display and collateral locally. If you have a local partner or reseller, contact it to see what display and/or collateral items it has on hand.

> **Show Smarts**
>
> Always travel with a CD or memory stick containing your display and collateral graphic files in case your booth does not arrive and you need to reprint graphics or collateral.

If your budget doesn't allow for reprinting or rental of a booth, then hold your head high and poke fun at your missing shipment! Create a handmade sign indicating the shipping mishap; include your company name and a few key benefits and attach it to the pipe and drape. Act like it is "business as usual" by engaging, qualifying, closing, and getting leads from attendees. You are sure to gain sympathy points.

But even if your budget is low, a couple of sign holders from a local office store, some rented furniture, or maybe a trip to the local IKEA can help you save the day at a minimal cost.

The Least You Need to Know

◆ Always know the weight of your shipment; you need that data to get quotes, check your bills, and even apply for insurance.

◆ Decide on appropriate shipping containers and have a packing checklist for each box, crate, or container you ship.

◆ Sloppy material handling forms can be expensive mistakes that result in forced freight, which is charged at a very high premium.

◆ The shipping weight is determined by whichever is heavier— actual weight or dimensional weight.

◆ If your booth doesn't arrive, consider renting a display from show services or purchasing some items from a discount furniture store.

◆ Always have electronic copies of your signage and collateral with you so that you can get extra copies printed if your material gets lost.

Chapter 16

Arrival and Setup

In This Chapter

- ◆ Arriving at the hotel and verifying that all staff members have arrived and are ready to go

- ◆ Managing the necessary planning documents to stay on top of your schedules and resources

- ◆ Managing your booth setup and dealing with emergencies such as missing booth parts or even a missing booth

- ◆ Holding mandatory meetings with all staff and required contractors to ensure flawless execution of the trade show plan

- ◆ Preparing public relations tasks, meetings, and events

You finally arrive in the show city, and your first stop is probably the hotel to unload bags and possibly change. If you are involved in setting up the booth, you may want to change that business suit into jeans and a T-shirt and then head over to the exhibition space.

The show floor buzzes with activity in a state of organized chaos, with forklifts moving materials around, labor setting up displays, show managers attending to booth details, and the occasional first-timer looking puzzled at the instructions that came with the pop-up display. It is a hectic day in the convention facility, but you probably feel some excitement to finally be at the show, setting up your display, presentations, and other materials. The general rule of thumb is the bigger and more complex your exhibit is, the sooner you want to be at the show.

Show Smarts

Make friends with the labor crew and your booth neighbors early. You may need something as simple as a screwdriver for setup, and borrowing one from your immediate booth neighborhood is easier than running to the hardware supply store. Bring some treats or promotional items from previous shows to use as thank you's!

If you have a large booth that requires significant setup time and large amounts of labor, you should arrive the day before setup begins. Even if you have a small and simple booth, don't arrive the morning of show day for setup. You need to leave yourself time to manage any emergencies that may occur during setup; you shouldn't expect everything to work flawlessly. In addition to setting up the booth, you'll have a number of other tasks on your plate such as getting press kits into the press room, confirming your staff's location, and confirming meetings.

Hotel Check-In

Once you get to the hotel, try to check in to your room, even if you arrive before official check-in times. If the hotel has a clean room in your category, it will allow you to check in early. The only possible exception to this is if you are an elite member of the hotel's frequent guest program that entitles you to upgrades when available. In that case, checking in before 3 P.M. frequently means that you will get a regular room because the upgraded rooms are not serviced yet.

If you can't check in yet, or choose not to, at least leave any luggage you don't need at the show with the bellhop so you are free to start your preshow preparations. Also while you are at the hotel, verify that all your staff members booked at the same hotel have confirmed reservations and that they all have a valid credit card on file to hold their rooms. Show hotels are often sold out, and you don't want one of your booth staffers to end up at a different hotel because of a missing credit card.

If you are lucky enough to arrive before the setup starts, use this opportunity to review show details and have a moment of rest; it might be your last one for quite a while.

Show Smarts

If one of your booth team members is an elite member in the hotel chain's frequent guest program, ask to keep one room for late checkout on the last day. That way, you have a room to store luggage or change in when you return from breakdown and get ready to leave.

Convention Facility

When it's time to start setting up, head over to the convention facility. If you followed my advice about using one of the closest hotels, this is probably just a short walk. You may end up taking a cab, though, if you brought any last-minute material that wasn't part of the show shipment.

The first thing you need to do once you arrive at the convention facility is head to registration to pick up your badge. It is almost certain that you will not be allowed access to the show floor unless you have your exhibitor badge. Some shows allow you to pick up exhibitor passes for all of your staff members, but in most cases they each must pick up their own.

Paperwork to Have with You

Don't forget to bring all the necessary paperwork. Your master show binder discussed in Chapter 4 should be your permanent companion during the setup phase and maybe even for the entire show. If people wouldn't look funny at you, I'd recommend handcuffing it to your wrist. It contains all your show-planning information including any extra events, media appointments, booth staff scheduling, executive scheduling, and networking events. It holds all the paperwork related to rentals, purchases, shipping, as well as copies of all agreements and contact information for anyone who could be remotely useful during the event.

If any emergencies such as nondeliveries or broken items arise, call the relevant company immediately and take notes on who you spoke with and what was discussed. Make sure you ask for an after-hours contact if your item is not received within their business hours. Also don't forget to request reimbursement for material handling fees if you receive a broken item.

Show Smarts

If there is a chance you might lose your binder, scan all your paperwork and put it on your hard drive as a backup before leaving for the show.

If you rented items from the show that are missing or have defects, simply visit the show services counter on the show floor. If you bring all your paperwork, you will most likely resolve the situation easily. They should have all materials on-site, so wait times should be very limited.

Picking Up Exhibitor and VIP Badges

When you pick up your badge, always ask if you can pick up badges for all booth staffers so that they don't have to wait in long lines when the show opens. Ask even if the show guide says they have to be picked up in person, especially if you are a repeat exhibitor and you know some of the show managers who hang around the registration area.

Show Smarts

Picking up VIP badges and having them in your possession enables a company executive or salesperson to meet the VIP personally to hand over the badge.

The same applies to picking up badges for VIPs, your media personnel, contractors, or others. It never hurts to ask. Some shows let you; others don't.

Booth Setup

Once you verify that your booth has arrived, it's time to turn all the bits and pieces into something presentable. Make sure you have your checklist of items to set up and have the setup team or setup labor check off each item as it is completed. Always have your booth map available to make sure everything is set up according to plan. With that said, though, now that you are on the floor and see the booth in its natural habitat for the first time, you may find it necessary to make some adjustments. This is not uncommon, and you should feel perfectly fine changing things as needed.

Make Sure Display Arrived

If your booth is small enough that you brought it with you, the suspense of whether it made it or not was over at the conveyor belt at the airport. But if you shipped your booth, one of the first things to do is find your display. Reading online that your shipment has been delivered is a good start, but seeing the boxes in good condition on your floor space for the first time boosts your confidence. So, after checking in and picking up badges, go to your booth to see if your shipment arrived.

If your booth is empty, check with the general contractor's service desk. Often they can locate your shipment; ask them to call the freight foreman to see if the shipping company driver has checked in. If he has, the foreman can also tell you where the driver currently is and provide an estimated time as to when the truck will be unloaded.

Contact Shipping Company

Now, if you find out that your booth has not arrived on the premises, call the shipping company for an update on your display's location. Always ask for an after-hour contact in case your booth does not materialize during regular business hours and you need to follow up late that day.

The worst-case scenario is that your booth will not arrive in time for the show or that it is damaged beyond hope for an easy and quick repair. If that happens, it is time to take a deep breath and go back to Chapter 15 of this book and its discussion on contingency planning and how to deal with a catastrophic event.

Show Smarts

Always ask the shipping company for the cell phone number of the driver if your booth is late. Cutting out the middle man during communications often greatly expedites things.

Check on Labor Team Setup

With a little bit of luck, you will get to your booth space and find not only that it has all arrived but that the labor team has already started the setup process. This, of course, applies only to bigger booths that aren't waiting for your own screwdriver skills to turn them into something resembling what you have in your trade show plan.

Although you should provide the labor team members with your cell phone number in case they have questions or there is an emergency, checking on their progress in person every so often is a good idea. There are hefty overtime charges for labor, so a company representative supervising setup and construction often speeds things up.

Setting Up by Booth Staff

Typical displays for 10'×10' or even 10'×20' booths can be assembled by you or your booth staffers, even in cities with strict union regulations. Whoever sets up your display must have access to a booth layout plan so that it is completely clear where each item goes. If you have a new display, make sure that all the necessary instructions are included and that staffers have access to an emergency contact at the display company in case they experience trouble assembling the display.

If part of your booth staff team is responsible for setup, you not only have to verify that the booth has arrived but also that your assembly team has. As with regular hired labor, things go more smoothly and expeditiously when supervised. If you have enough staff members, it's a good idea to have one group of people set up the booth and another one break it down, enabling you to distribute those duties better.

Checking That All Equipment Is Working

Regardless of whether your audio-visual equipment is set up by booth staff or the show's audio-visual company, be sure to personally verify that all equipment is configured and working correctly. Deal with any functional problems immediately.

Once all equipment is set up and ready to go, perform a "dry run" of your video presentations and any associated equipment. If you do a live presentation with a microphone and speakers, have the performer practice with the equipment to make sure he or she is comfortable with it. Make sure at least two people know how to operate everything and that everything is working as expected.

While every show provides some flavor of security, I recommend taking critical, high-value items from the floor overnight. If you do this, make sure that all staff members know how to reconnect, set up, and run the equipment again before the show opens.

Show Smarts

If you use an electronic lead system, check that it works properly by doing several tests with your own badge. Fill in a few leads completely, including notes, and save them to complete a test.

Check Your Lighting

If lighting is part of your exhibit, test that equipment as well. Make sure the lighting does not distract from any presentation you have and that it does not create a glare. If you use a live presenter, make sure the light does not distract from that person. Make any necessary adjustments to fix the problems you find. While the weight of your master trade show binder may suggest otherwise, none of your plan components is written in stone. You should always feel free to make adjustments when circumstances change.

Show Services Desk Offers Help

The show services desk, typically located on the show floor, can provide you with help before and during the show. It is usually located out of sight but close enough to be easily accessible. Usually, all service companies have a representative available to speak with and attend to any problems. There are very few exceptions to this.

In addition to helping with existing orders and services, you can order on-site services as well, but expect to pay a significant premium for anything ordered during the show.

Meetings: Hired Staff and Booth Staff

As discussed earlier in the book, it is important to have regular meetings with your booth staffers and other hired help such as speakers, consultants, and local receptionists. Set the meeting times well in advance and hold the earlier ones at the booth so that everyone becomes familiar with all its features and functions. Prepare a checklist or agenda of items and spend the meeting time effectively. Cover booth staff training items again now that you are in the booth. For example, conduct role-playing in the actual environment where interactions happen. Practice lead capture, note taking, and other important items.

While some of your staffers may disagree, you cannot cover booth staff schedules, networking events, and your schedule often enough. These meetings are also good opportunities to remind booth staff of the media contact process and to reiterate the show goals. If you have consultants or other temporary team members helping during the show, this is a good opportunity to introduce them to your regular staff.

Your Public Relations Tasks

If you manage your public relations tasks yourself, you have a lot of activities to perform while at the show. Always have a show guide with an exhibit facility map and all media contact info available in your show binder. As previously mentioned, only extreme circumstances such as death or civil unrest should separate you from your show binder; carry it with you at all times. It includes the company spokesperson's schedule, which is important to have if a media contact needs to reschedule, which happens quite frequently. Having all the information you need at your fingertips saves time and often avoids lost opportunities.

Public relations tasks are a big responsibility. Never forget that this is your company's opportunity to build personal relationships with media contacts that may result in a great deal of coverage for your company and products in the future. If possible, always ask important media contacts to join you for a meal or other activities outside the show to further build your relationship.

Press Kits: Press Room and Booth

Bring an ample supply of paper-based PR kits in folders or CDs with available materials to hand to media contacts. Have enough for the press room as well as your booth. Locate the press room on your first trip to the convention center, and place media kits in the press room. This gives media contacts that you are not scheduled to see the ability to learn more about your company and products. Always have your booth number on your materials as well as a contact number where you or your media person can be reached during the show. That way, a reporter can either stop by the booth or call if he or she is interested in arranging a meeting while at the show.

The main benefit of using CDs is that if media contacts want to include parts of the materials in an article, they can copy and paste it using the CD. The easier you make their job, the more likely you are to get coverage. Bring a press kit to meetings with media contacts, or ask if they want it sent to them after the show. The odds that they will keep the kit go up when you send it after the show. Quite often, before members of the media leave the show, they dump all their materials on the hotel room floor and sort through them, deciding what to bring back with them. I am sure it doesn't surprise you to learn that most of it ends up in the garbage.

Managing Media Appointments

Make it a rule to always review information about the reporter with your company spokesperson before any media appointments. Everyone from your company attending the meeting needs to know the reporter's publication, the topics it covers, recent articles it has featured, and upcoming articles relevant to your company where you might be a reference or a source.

When you are at the appointment, pay attention to the conversation and make sure it stays on topic. Golfing, French food, and the Olympics might be interesting

Show Smarts

If you have meetings with media representatives who are unfamiliar with your company spokesperson, prepare a briefing folder containing key information about the reporter as well as copies of a couple recent articles.

topics and may help build a relationship, but they do not educate the reporter about your business.

Your company spokesperson should be well trained and experienced enough to manage these situations, but you should redirect a conversation if you feel it necessary. Of course, in a smaller company, you may be the spokesperson.

The Least You Need to Know

- ◆ Check in to your hotel before going to the convention facility, and make sure arrangements are made to hold rooms for any staff that needs a late check-in.

- ◆ The first thing to do after arriving at the convention facility is pick up your badge because you aren't allowed on the show floor without it.

- ◆ Once you have your badge, head to the booth to make sure your shipment has arrived and setup has begun on larger displays or that you or your booth staff is prepared to set up a smaller display.

- ◆ Once the booth is set up, check all equipment and perform test runs of presentations; make sure all booth staffers know how to operate and activate equipment.

- ◆ Have a training session in the booth with staff members and any additional hired staff to go over all show-related items, including items covered in preshow training sessions and role-playing in the booth with the actual equipment.

- ◆ Have your public relations schedule with you at all times and make sure all staff members are aware of the media process—most important, what to say and what not to say to media contacts.

Chapter 17

Core Show Days

In This Chapter

- ◆ Manage booth staff and maximize productivity to reach or exceed show goals
- ◆ Use showtime to gather competitive information
- ◆ Hold daily status meetings to immediately identify and correct issues
- ◆ Get through the show without burning out

Months of hard work researching shows and developing your show strategy and marketing plan were all done in anticipation of "the big event," and now you're finally here. The booth is set up, and your staffers are eager and ready to go. It's showtime!

This chapter outlines the activities you need to oversee during show days and how to make sure your booth staff is at the top of its game. Once the lights turn on, the exhibit doors open, and the attendees swarm in, it is your job to make sure everyone stays focused and follows the guidelines you outlined.

Your Tasks During Show Hours

Your main tasks during the show depend on how many hats you wear at the show. The number of hats directly relates to the size of your company. The smaller the company, the more numerous the tasks and activities you do yourself. Your trade show plan defines what you have to do and when you have to do it, whether it is working the booth, coaching your booth staff, or being out of the booth entirely for PR and other event activities.

Evaluate and Help Booth Staff

Regardless of why you are in the booth—whether it's to work or to observe—you have to pay close attention to your booth staff's behavior and how closely they follow their qualification and lead-capture-process training. Any deviation has to be corrected immediately. A delay of just a few minutes can mean several lost qualified leads.

Listen to the conversations between your booth staff members and attendees. Observe how they engage, qualify, and close leads. If you hear things that require immediate attention, wait for the booth staffer to finish his current conversation and then pull him quietly away from the booth to discuss what he should or shouldn't be saying. Position yourself as a teacher and be firm about what needs to be done to reach the show goals. Have a postshow meeting every day to discuss the day and review how close you are to reaching your goals. Ask for suggestions to improve things and bring up your own as needed.

> **Don't Do It!**
>
> Don't point fingers at individual booth staffers during your daily show meetings. Keep your advice general and repeat the expected behavior.

Manage Collateral and Giveaway Inventory

One part of your job at the show is to make sure you always have an adequate supply of collateral and promotional items available. Remember that there is a material handling fee every time you access your show-accessible storage, so try to have enough material for the entire day.

Budget Savers

As a reminder, consider storing collateral and inventory in your hotel room with any overflow in booth staffers' rooms. Have a cart with you and bring enough materials for the day to avoid the hefty material handling fees to get items from accessible storage (see Chapter 4).

Make Sure Equipment Runs Smoothly

Each day of the show, you or the booth staffers on duty should arrive at least half an hour before the show opens to verify that all equipment is set up, functioning, and ready to go. Verify that all booth staffers know how to properly use all equipment.

Manage Any Emergencies

Even the best-planned show has some unexpected occurrences. Make sure all your booth staffers have your cell phone number so they can reach you during emergencies. Leave a copy of your schedule for the day with your booth staffers so that they know what times you are in media meetings, holding seminars, or are otherwise unavailable. Always designate someone as a backup decision maker or "booth captain" for times when you are unavailable, and make sure that individual knows where to get help such as from show services.

Show Smarts

Make sure all booth staffers have their schedule, which should list all of their booth hours and other activities they are scheduled to attend.

Gather Information

Even though you have read this book and are well prepared for your show, you should take the time to walk the show floor and look for ideas for future shows. Bring a digital camera so you can take pictures of creative displays, themes, or promotional items. Collect samples of collateral material that is particularly well done. Put these items into what I like to call "inspiration files."

Booth Staff

Your booth staffers should be well prepared and know exactly what their booth hours are and what other activities they are scheduled to attend based on the "Booth Staff Guide" you provided. Every single team member has a lot of responsibility during the show, and everyone's contribution counts toward achieving the show goals.

Booth Duty

Because you created booth staff schedules based on staffers' skills and knowledge complementing each other, it is important not to allow the staffers to trade shifts without your approval. Each booth staffer is responsible for being early, wearing the appropriate attire, and following the rules and procedures learned during booth staff training. Each team member should have individual goals and should understand how he or she contributes toward achieving the overall show goals.

Show Smarts _____

Being on time and in the booth during scheduled hours is a key responsibility of all your booth staffers. Provide an incentive such as a gift card for "perfect booth attendance" to make sure everyone shows up on time.

Client and Prospect Meetings

Booth staff members from the sales group should have a number of meetings already set up from their preshow activities. Your booth staff schedule should allow for additional meeting times for hot leads when decision makers are available.

If you don't have meeting space in your booth, be careful that meetings don't turn into excuses to avoid booth duty. Monitor results closely to avoid abuse. Make sure your sales staff is dressed appropriately for the occasion.

Networking

All your team members should have a networking plan that includes all scheduled events they are expected to attend. Remind them to review their networking goals before each event and to bring with them the networking cheat sheet developed in Chapter 9. Remind everyone of the dress code specific to each networking event and discuss their event experiences and successes during your daily exhibit staff meetings.

Touch Base with the Office

It is important to stay in touch with the office and check e-mail and voicemail at least once a day. Each staff member should do this. The business world doesn't stop just because you are out of town at a trade show. Check in to make sure leads are being received and processed and address any concerns that come up.

Don't Do It!

Every booth staff member should have time to check in with the office and answer important e-mails. Doing this in the booth during show hours, however, is not acceptable. Ban cell phone and personal digital assistant (PDA) usage on the show floor as much as possible.

Competitors at the Show

If some of your competitors are exhibiting at the same show, use the opportunity to gather information about them and their exhibits. If possible, take pictures of their booths, get collateral, and observe their booth etiquette and qualification process.

This is not something you should do while wearing your corporate logo shirt. If you want to experience the entire booth as a prospect, you may want to get an attendee badge with a different name and postal and e-mail addresses so that you can observe any follow-up activities. If you are too well known, send a junior member of your team or consider hiring a mystery shopper. In either case, document the findings for your postshow follow-up report, discussed in Chapter 20.

Comparing Booths and Show Floor Presence

Compare each competitor's booth attributes such as size and type of display. Pay attention to the look and feel of the booth. Is it spacious or crowded? Observe attendee traffic and note how long attendees stay in the booth.

Products Displayed

Make a list of all the products or services displayed at each competitor's booth. Take note of all similarities and differences when comparing your product and product positioning to theirs. If possible, get a demo of their product and get a feel for their booth staff's level of knowledge. Ask how their product compares to your product and evaluate their answer.

Collateral and Promotional Items

If your competitor provides promotional items, find out what it takes to get one. In particular, how qualified does an attendee have to be to get one, and what qualification process is used?

Take note of any games or raffles organized at the booth and if any qualification was required to participate. Investigate what types of collateral are available, where in the booth they are located, and if they are publicly accessible or you have to talk to a booth staffer to get them.

Booth Staff and Lead Qualifying

First observe what, if anything, invites you into the booth. If you enter the booth without being engaged, how long does it take before someone approaches you to assist? Evaluate the booth staffers' experience. Were they helpful and knowledgeable? Did they follow a lead-qualifying process, or were they more interested in collecting as many names as possible? Did they use the lead-collection system offered by the show, or did they have their own readers and software? Did they only collect business cards? Did the booth staff take notes of prospects' needs and requirements?

Special Events Held by Competitors

Make a list of all special events organized by competitors and see if you can find a way for you or someone else to attend and evaluate them. Also note what, if any, show-organized events they sponsored and what type of sponsorship it was.

Show Smarts

It might be difficult to attend competitor events yourself. Many times, however, resellers or distributors of your company's products attend those events. Most of them will share interesting details if you ask.

Using Mystery Shoppers to Visit Competitors

If you hire mystery shoppers to visit your competitors' booths, their trade show badges need to be ready with a fictitious company name. The e-mail address and postal address registered with the badge should go to a location where you can see their follow-up process. For obvious reasons, don't use the address of your business.

Most mystery shoppers have limited knowledge about the industry and products they are expected to investigate. Before they enter the show, meet with them to go over the information you want them to collect and what questions you want them to ask. Make sure they have enough background information to appear credible. In my experience, it works best if your mystery shoppers have a low-level, fictitious job title. This enables them to explain that their boss sent them there to gather information, providing an easy excuse if they don't understand unexpected qualifying questions. Give them a list of companies to visit and a booth map showing the locations. I strongly recommend preparing a report template for them to complete so that the reports follow the same format for each competitor visited.

Daily Status Meeting

Hold a daily meeting to discuss the progress toward your show goals and to address any issues that may arise. Present lead numbers and how they track toward the overall show goals. If you are behind schedule, solicit input from your team as to why that is. Ask for feedback on show hours and staffing to see if there are any peak times where booth traffic becomes too busy for the scheduled team members to handle.

Discuss the quality of attendees and how they match the advertised attendee description of the show prospectus. If staff members are not reporting for duty on time, address it in each meeting. If possible, hold this meeting after the show ends each day when things are fresh in everyone's mind. However, networking events and other scheduled items may not always make this timing possible. You may also have to organize more than one meeting if your staff size is large and shifts can't meet together.

Don't Do It!

Don't wait for the daily meeting to address issues that require more immediate attention, such as problems with the lead-qualification process. Every hour that a problem exists can cost you a large number of qualified leads.

In addition to discussing show floor status, have each staff member who attended a networking or media event summarize the highlights of that event.

Leads

Each evening, spend some time evaluating the leads from that day. Use that data for your progress report for the next day's meeting. Check on the quality of prospects entering the booth and how they meet the expected profiles. Verify each day that the lead-collection process works and that all qualifying questions are answered and tracked.

Look over the notes your booth staffers have been taking and make sure they make sense. Speak to any staffer who takes poor notes. Finally, follow the predetermined lead-handling process, which may include uploading them to your CRM system, e-mailing a spreadsheet, or simply mailing them back to the office for manual entering.

Show Smarts

Many companies spend significant amounts of money and resources getting new leads back to the office as quickly as possible. In many cases, though, that speed does not help much because the contact is often out of the office at the trade show. Following up the week after the show typically has a much higher connect ratio and better utilizes the time of your sales force. Think about this when deciding how quickly leads need to be sent to the office.

Avoid Burnout

Trade shows often have relentless schedules that are tiring for both attendees and exhibitors. Numerous event parties interfere with sleep schedules as well. You don't want zombies staffing your booth on the last day, so make sure everyone has some downtime and enough time to sleep. The closest hotels to the show are often the most expensive, but there is tremendous value in them being only across the street. Their proximity provides staffers the opportunity to get rest for an hour or two during shift breaks.

The Least You Need to Know

- ◆ Track and evaluate your progress toward reaching your show goals and make adjustments where needed.

- ◆ Use the opportunities the show offers to gather information about your direct and indirect competitors.

- ◆ Deal with any issues as quickly as possible; a flaw in your process or a faulty machine can cost you many qualified leads per hour.

- ◆ Maximize your time, but don't push yourself or your staffers to the point of exhaustion.

Chapter 18

Final Day and Cleanup

In This Chapter

- Using the last day to maximize time with attendees
- Determining the right time to pack up and break down the booth
- Knowing what to expect during the breakdown time
- Helping your staff pack up and prepare things for the next show
- Making sure to avoid costly forced freight

The close of a show is almost as hectic as the final preparations, except that now you are no longer excited—just exhausted. Your desire to "get out of there" the moment the exhibit hall closes its doors can be strong, but that thought process can breed costly mistakes. From forgetting a laptop to damaging the display to forgetting to complete important forms, there are plenty of opportunities for things to go wrong. If you are breaking down the booth yourself, everyone in your team is probably anxious to get the job done and leave, but this is not a time to rush.

The last day is also not the day to stark slacking off at the booth. Traffic is usually lighter on the last day, but that creates a great opportunity to spend extra time with attendees that you would not have had available on any other show day. Also a special promotion can keep the booth busy at a time when a significant number of attendees are already on their way to the airport.

Attracting Attendees to the Booth

The closer you get to the show's closing, the more abandoned the show floor appears. Consider special price drawings in the late hours of the last day with an incentive related to your company, for example one year of free service or a free product. It has to be something that is only attractive to people in your target audience.

> **Don't Do It!**
>
> Using gimmicks to draw traffic, such as giving away big-ticket items like an expensive TV, generates a lot of interest in your booth. The people being drawn in, however, may not be in your target audience or have any need for your product. Keep this in mind and offer promotional items that will draw qualified attendees to your booth.

Spending More Time with Attendees

The attendees you do attract to your booth on the last day receive more attention because of staff availability. The traffic management techniques you employ the first days of the show are designed to capture all relevant attendee information and then get them to move on. The traffic management techniques for the last day are different; you want people to stay longer now.

Living near Miami, I often have the opportunity to watch people in a pedestrian area of South Beach that is lined with restaurants. Every evening most of those restaurants are pretty full, but a couple of them have lots of space available. The majority of people walking around looking for dinner are tourists, and most of them stop at the restaurants that are already busy rather than go to the ones without lines.

Most humans find comfort in groups. A busy, populated booth looks interesting; an empty one looks scary. Keeping attendees at your booth attracts additional ones. The last day is the day to answer more exotic questions and do more detailed demonstrations than you would otherwise.

At the same time, though, do not dominate attendees' time; pay attention to signals from attendees suggesting that they want to move on but don't want to be rude. Allow them time to ask as many questions as they want, but don't try to hold them hostage. It's not a bad idea to mention to attendees throughout the show that the last day is typically slower. Invite them back when you will have time to give them more personalized attention. Be sure to update any notes on the prospect.

When to "Break Down" the Booth

Often you will find exhibitors starting to pack up 15 minutes or more before the show closes. Don't follow their lead. Neal Shact, a good friend of mine who taught me an awful lot about networking events, once told me, "A networking event isn't over 'til the last drunk has left." Something similar holds true for trade shows; they are not over until the last attendee has left the exhibit hall. Don't break down until the show floor closes, which is typically 5 to 10 minutes after the official closing time. Dismantling your booth makes a bad impression on attendees still strolling the aisles, plus you never know what last lead you might miss.

Close of Show Activity to Expect

If you have never witnessed it before, the speed at which a glamorous hall full of displays, people, sounds, and light turns into an empty concrete hall will amaze you. Less than two hours after the show closes, almost everything resembling a trade show disappears into boxes, on its way to a warehouse for the next event.

Once the last visitor has left, laborers swarm like ants onto the floor to dismantle everything. Even if you have a small 10'×10' booth to dismantle, the floor carpet disappears and the pipes and drapes are collected before you pack the last of your items into the shipping container.

Because show services rolls up the aisle carpet well before you finish packing up, make sure to keep it clear. You will also see forklifts driving by, moving the first fully packed crates toward the loading docks.

Show Smarts

Never list the contents of a box on the outside; it makes it easier for thieves to find the valuable items.

Have a content list in the show binder and in the electronic file. This helps track supplies that need to be replenished.

Packing Up Procedure

You may have to wait a little bit for show services to bring your containers to your booth, but they are normally very fast. This is one of the few times in the service industry when you can almost always count on it being done much quicker than promised. They often claim you may have to wait 2 to 12 hours, depending on the size of the show. Most of the time, though, your material is delivered in under an hour. While you wait for your boxes, start breaking down the display and other booth items so that you are ready the moment your shipping containers arrive.

Show Smarts

Make sure to remove old labels and clearly label all boxes and crates with the shipping address. It's always a good idea to place multiple labels on several sides of the crate.

Each staff member has individual instructions; everyone knows what to do. Once the crates arrive, staff members pack the items they are responsible for. When all crates are packed, leave them properly labeled in the booth where show services will pick them up. You can, of course, wait for that, but it really is a waste of your time.

Using Staff Effectively to Pack Up

As mentioned in Chapter 16, if you have enough staff, have a team for setup and a separate team for breakdown. This not only helps distribute the work fairly, it also makes travel arrangements easier because you never want all of your staff stuck with the same travel problem.

To make the breakdown as smooth and efficient as possible, give each staff member specific tasks to complete. Tasks can be broken down into portions as in this example: Jim and Sam dismantle the display, Sally packs all supplies and collateral, Mike dismantles all electronics. The bottom line is to give each staffer a description of his or her duties and your expectations. For example, you may want Sally to count the supplies and collateral so that you know whether items need to be purchased for subsequent shows.

Packing Materials: Procedure for Staff

Prepare a checklist for each shipping box for each show. Using that list, staff members should check off each item they pack and alert everyone to look for missing items around the booth. When items cannot be found, mark them as lost so that they can be replaced before the next show.

Use the checklists to keep appropriate items together. Designate areas within your booth space for specific shipping boxes, keeping everything out of the aisles. There are a lot of forklifts bringing and removing crates during breakdown. Pay attention to the activity in the aisle. You don't want your staff hurt or your items damaged.

Show Smarts

A checklist not only helps your staff pack the correct items into the correct box, it becomes a great supply-management tool for the show manager. Back in the office, use the checklist to see how much collateral was used and what supplies you need to order.

Material Handling

Hopefully, you followed my advice and arranged for shipping preshow. If this is the case, you know what shipping company is picking up your items, so include that information on the material handling forms. If you submitted the form for preprinted material handling forms and shipping labels, you don't need to complete any additional forms. You only have to go to show services, pick them up, and stick them on your shipping containers.

On the other hand, if you overlooked prearranging your shipping, it can be arranged through the show carrier at the show services desk. Of course, there is a premium to be paid for this.

For every box or container shipped, a material handling form needs to be completed indicating to show services which shipping company will be picking up your crates and cases. Once completed, hand the form(s) to show services at the close of show. They then make the necessary arrangements to move the items from your booth, typically by forklift, to the loading dock and out to your shipping company.

In most cases, show services delivers material handling forms to your booth before the show closes. If you have not received the forms, go to the show services desk to ask for them. You can usually get blank shipping labels there also, should you need any. Remember that show services charges a material handling fee to transport the items. If you send a shipment, this is something you are required to pay. Even if you have only a couple of items you could carry, you cannot bring them to the loading dock yourself.

Show Smarts

If you don't have shipping labels, a plain piece of paper works. Indicate on the paper where the shipment comes from (the exhibit hall address), where it is going, when it should arrive, who the carrier is, and how many pieces there are altogether. For example, write number 1 of 7 pieces, number 2 of 7 pieces, and so on. Place these handmade labels on each piece (in several areas) to be shipped and tape them over with clear packing tape several times.

Avoiding Forced Freight

Forced freight is something you should avoid at all costs. These exorbitant shipping fees are assessed for several reasons.

The following is a short list of common reasons why you end up with forced freight, though I do not claim this list is complete.

- ◆ A material handling form is not filled in or not handed back to show services.

- The shipping carrier is not indicated on the material handling form turned in to show services.

- Show services can't read the handwriting on the form.

- Your shipping company does not check in by the scheduled time indicated in the exhibitor kit.

def•i•ni•tion

Forced freight becomes an issue when there are problems with your material handling form. Show services must comply with an agreed-upon schedule with the show hall regarding the removal of all items from the facility. If there are problems with your material handling form, the show organizers remove your items from the show floor themselves to meet the mandated deadline. The items are then sent either to the show services warehouse or to you, both of which will cost you a significant premium.

If the shipping company was not indicated on the form or the shipping company missed the check-in time, your items may still be shipped to the address on the material handling form. In other cases, your items may be sent to the show services warehouse for holding. If that happens, you have to pay storage fees and material handling fees until you clear things up and get the items on the way to their true destination.

The bottom line is this: forced freight is incredibly costly, and you should do everything humanly possible to avoid it.

The following guidelines should help:

- Always check the exhibitor kit for the option to fill in a form preshow that prints the material handling form from a computer at the show. This also provides you with shipping labels that you simply have to pick up at the show services desk (as previously mentioned), avoiding any handwriting issues.

- Have your shipping company confirm the check-in time in writing. You can then hold it accountable for financial damages if its driver checks in late.

- List the shipping company you use for your outbound shipment on the material handling form.

♦ If the material handling form is not completed preshow, make sure someone with very clear handwriting fills in the form.

♦ Review the material handling form for accuracy. Ask show services if it is filled in completely. Record the name of the show person you speak to and what branch of the company he or she is from in your planning binder.

Carefully Review Accuracy of Billing Statements

Verify the final invoices from show services for accuracy as soon as possible. Make sure all invoiced items match up with services actually performed, such as material handling charges, items ordered for the booth, and accessible storage. You can ask for a preliminary copy while at the show, but additional charges for material handling and possibly forced freight are pending at this point. Immediately dispute any initial discrepancies you notice on-site; have your show planning binder available to show proof of any oversights. The show handles a large number of exhibitors, and billing mistakes are not uncommon. Review your invoices carefully. Material handling charges are based on weight, so it is very important to know the weight of your items. Otherwise, you have little to go on when it comes to checking the accuracy of those charges.

The Least You Need to Know

♦ Use the last day of the show to your advantage and spend more time with attendees while the show floor is quieter. Invite qualified prospects that stay to the last day back to the booth and offer incentives for attendees to come back on the last day.

♦ Break down the booth after the announcement that the show floor is closed and all attendees have left the hall. Don't start earlier even if other booths do. It's unprofessional, and you may miss potentially valuable opportunities.

◆ Assign booth staff members tasks to pack up the display and booth materials. Give them checklists to use to make sure they pack all items. Have them count supply and collateral items as they pack so that you know quantities for tracking purposes and potential ordering.

◆ Make sure the material handling form is filled in completely, that your shipping company is listed on the form, and that the delivery address is written legibly. Mistakes or omissions on the material handling form are the usual reason for forced freight charges, which you want to avoid.

◆ Check show billing carefully for accuracy because errors are common. Many exhibitors simply accept and pay invoices because they are confused by them, particularly material handling charges. Always know the weight of your shipment and be savvy about understanding charges.

◆ Expect heightened activity everywhere on the show floor once breakdown begins and be extra careful of forklifts and carts buzzing through aisles. It happens fast; be prepared for this, especially if exhibiting for the first time.

Part 5

Postshow

Before you started reading this book, you might have thought you'd be done with the trade show on the last day of the show. Unfortunately, that is not quite the case.

Now is the time for marketing and sales to follow up on the sales leads and turn your trade show efforts into revenue. You also have to follow up with any media contacts you met, which is important because positive articles covering your company or products not only give you a third-party endorsement, they also typically accelerate the sales cycle. Finally, even if you followed all the advice in this book, there will probably still be areas where you can improve. Postshow time is when you sum it all up and figure out what worked and what didn't so that you can do it even better next time.

Chapter 19

Turning Trade Show Efforts into Sales

In This Chapter

- ◆ Optimizing follow-up timelines for leads to achieve the best possible result
- ◆ Tracking your follow-up progress of leads and media contacts
- ◆ Sending targeted materials to both prospects and media contacts
- ◆ Using media coverage to enhance conversion speed
- ◆ Using automated marketing techniques to simplify the lead follow-up process

As you've discovered, it takes a lot of effort to organize the show and collect those targeted leads the sales organization craves. Chapter 13 covered preshow planning for leads; this chapter takes it a step further and covers how to optimize the follow-up process for both sales leads and media contacts. This is another area—not surprisingly—that requires some thought and planning to be successful. The primary goals are to beat out the competition and minimize company resources in the follow-up process.

Assigning Leads

Although a number of follow-up activities are automated, there are activities that require direct contact between salespeople and specific leads. This means you need rules in place regarding who gets what leads. It really shouldn't be your responsibility to tell the sales organization how to distribute leads, but a clearly defined, well-understood process should be in place. While you want to avoid arguments within the sales team, you also don't want your top leads receiving calls from every member of the sales team. If you have to get involved in lead assignment, I suggest the *round-robin* method in which each sales member is assigned leads in a circular order starting with the top leads. That way, everyone gets a fair share with equal opportunity.

def•i•ni•tion

Round robin is a simple algorithm that gives each resource the same priority and assigns tasks in sequential order between resources. Does that still sound complicated? Think of a stack of cards that is dealt to a fixed number of players. In circular order, the dealer distributes cards to all players until no cards are left. The algorithm that describes this card-dealing process is round robin.

International Leads

If you exhibited at a larger show, you probably collected some leads from prospects that are not domestic. If you only have one sales organization at one location, you probably treat those leads like any other. But if you have offices or distributors in the region where the prospect resides, you may want to remove those leads from the general pool and hand them over to the organization best suited for follow-up. If you do transfer the leads to an

Show Smarts

If you collect a fair number of international leads that you hand off to partners or international sales offices, make sure to follow up with those organizations to see what becomes of them for your postshow reporting.

international office or regional partner, brief the team about the event where the lead was collected as well as the meaning of any notes or scores.

Competitor Leads

Just as I encouraged you to check out your competitors, your competitors may have come to check you out. If you notice a competitor in your leads, simply mark that lead closed so that no follow-up occurs. There is no need to send helpful information to your competition.

Following Up with Leads

Before you kick off your main follow-up campaign, it is a good idea to meet with the sales team to provide show details and the lead-generation process at the booth. Review the attendee profiles. Explain how the leads were collected, scored, and managed. Of course, if all your salespeople were at the show, you can safely skip this meeting. What is important is that every sales team member understands how the leads were generated, how to read and interpret any notes, and the scoring process.

Timeframe for Following Up

The lead follow-up process depends on your sales manpower and the technical resources available for automated follow-ups. In general, make the first follow-up contact within five business days of the show closing, either by postal mail, e-mail, or telephone. If you have the technical ability, an e-mail follow-up with some additional data sheets or special show offers is a good idea. Some companies begin the follow-up process this way on the day the lead is collected at the show. While that creates an impression of efficiency, the value is questionable because studies show that a majority of trade show attendees read only critical e-mail during their show days and delete or ignore mail that is not important. My advice, assuming you have the technical capability, is to send a courtesy e-mail the day you collect the lead, thanking the attendee for visiting your booth and informing him that your company will follow up shortly after the show. That way, if your mail gets noticed, your company stays in the visitor's mind, and you don't risk him deleting important content you want him to have. Your first serious attempt to follow up with a prospect and work on conversion should take place the week after the show—and not until the middle of that week to give the prospect enough time to catch up on office work. Your sales cycles, resources, and capabilities determine how you contact your prospect and what information you provide.

Scoring-Based Follow-Up

Now that the sales organization has to prioritize leads, our efforts to score them come into play. The highest scoring leads are processed first when it comes to follow-up calls. The higher the lead score, the sooner the call attempt is made. (Of course, with an automated e-mail as first contact, they are all treated the same.) Developing an optimized conversion and sales cycle goes well beyond the scope of this book. Suffice it to say that any such process that your company applies to leads generated by other means is applicable to trade show leads.

Sending Materials to Prospects

Within 7 to 10 days of the show, the follow-up material you created in advance of the show is sent to the prospects. You may have designed different material and different sales follow-up processes based on lead scores. If you have more than one product or more than one application for it, you also have different follow-up materials targeted at the prospect's specific needs. As with any messaging you do, it is as targeted as possible.

Follow-Up E-Mail

E-mail is typically the easiest, fastest, and cheapest way to follow up. Because you collected the contacts as leads and were provided e-mail addresses for follow-up purposes, you do not have to be concerned about legal issues such as the CANSPAM Act, which regulates the sending of commercial e-mail. That doesn't mean every booth attendee has agreed to be part of your newsletter from now on. Use e-mail in moderation, and while adding lead contacts to a newsletter is not a bad idea, make sure recipients have an easy way to opt out.

Show Smarts

If you chose to send e-mails as part of your follow-up process, don't let them get swallowed up by common junk e-mail filters. Although it's simple and not foolproof, I recommend using Microsoft Outlook combined with the most current junk e-mail updates to test receiving your messages and see if they get filtered. Work on them until they get through. To make this a valid test, you must send them to or from an address outside the corporate e-mail server.

Follow-Up Sales Letter

Although it's more expensive, the paper mailing of a follow-up letter is often received better and gains more attention. Tools like Mail Merge in Microsoft Word make it easy to send personalized letters to large numbers of people. You can even use Microsoft Word and services such as Stamps.com to print the letter, envelope, and postage. It is, of course, a matter of volume, but if possible have the respective salespeople personally sign the letters sent in their name. This adds a great level of personalization to it and makes a much stronger impression than a letter without a signature or with a printed one. Depending on your industry and audience, you may also want to send out collateral with your letter.

Follow-Up Collateral

Sending additional collateral with your follow-up mailing, whether it is paper mail or electronic, is often a good idea. If you go that route, the additional collateral should not be the same generic information provided at the show; it should be specific to the needs and qualification criteria recorded as part of the lead information.

Collateral for the higher scoring leads should include more targeted data sheets, case studies, and *white papers*. A more generic, brochure type of collateral might be in order for leads that qualified lower.

def•i•ni•tion

White papers are reports or guides that are written to educate people about specific problems and how to resolve them. They are designed to help with a decision-making process and are commonly used in business and politics.

Follow-Up Survey

Consider sending out a survey if you are interested in market research or if you want to measure the effectiveness of your booth or other exhibit components.

The easier you make the survey, the more likely the recipients are to respond. Consequently, break everything down into multiple-choice questions and pay attention to the length of your survey.

Studies show a sharp decline in completed surveys when they take more than six minutes to complete. If you think your survey is close to that length, have a couple of friends or co-workers answer your survey and time them. Reduce the number of questions if the average completion time is above five minutes. As you might know, providing an incentive improves response rates. But be careful with any prize drawings. While rarely enforced, there are a number of state laws complicating what can and cannot be done as part of a prize drawing. If you want to be on the safe side, consult a specialized attorney before proceeding.

Show Smarts

There are several software packages and reasonably priced survey services that make this an easy and cost-efficient process to implement. If the number of intended recipients is large, consider a service because its mail system specializes in working around spam filters, providing you a higher percentage of delivered messages.

Tracking Communications with Leads

Each lead needs to be entered into some type of database. If the numbers aren't too big, a shared Excel spreadsheet works, but contact management software such as ACT!, Microsoft Business Contact Manager, or even better, a full-fledged CRM solution such as Salesforce.com or Microsoft CRM, which are more powerful and offer more flexible options. Every incoming and outgoing communication regarding a lead needs to be recorded so that information can be used for follow-up and reporting.

Customer Relationship Management Programs

We've already talked about several of the benefits inherent to contact management software or customer relationship management (CRM) software. Recording every single contact you have with a lead and then generating a variety of reports about those contacts has tremendous value. Those software applications enable you to rate the probability of closing the sale, which leads to increasingly accurate forecasting of sales numbers.

Contact management software is typically a single desktop-type application that is installed on one or more PCs, possibly with basic network functionality such as the ability to synchronize data between computers. CRM software is almost always a client/server-based software, meaning you have a central database that is accessed by the various software clients. In addition to traditional software applications, CRM solutions are increasingly available as an outsourced, web-hosted solution. Setting up a CRM solution is a complex and often painful process, making hosted solutions an interesting alternative. Any of those solutions should enable management to run customized reports tracking progress on initiatives such as tradeshows or other marketing programs.

Automated Marketing to Leads

All CRM software and a variety of more basic software applications enable automated marketing to leads. Customized collateral and letters are preloaded. The software follows a preprogrammed cause of action that, depending on the type of product or service you sell, can follow through all the way to an online purchase.

Automated marketing is a great way to stay in touch with prospects without additional work. As with newsletters, however, you need to provide a way for recipients to opt out from continuously receiving messages.

Media Contacts

Positive media coverage has two primary benefits. The first is that it results in new leads, like an advertisement in a publication. The other benefit is third-party validation, which is the most valuable part. It makes a big difference if you are the one saying, "My product is great," or if a renowned publication is saying, "This product is great." You get paid to make these statements, while almost everybody thinks the media provides impartial reviews.

Utilize both benefits to generate more sales, and with a publication having validated your product, your sales cycles will often be shorter. Given the importance and value of media coverage, any media leads generated during the show deserve their own, highly personalized follow-up process. If you have a PR agency, the vast majority of this work is done by it. This section is designed for those readers who do not have a PR agency available and who do the leg work themselves. Media contacts are VIPs for your organization and should be treated as such. Find out how and when they like to be contacted, and respect their wishes as much as possible. Always be extra courteous. When you call, ask if now is a good time to talk, and agree on a different time if it's inconvenient now.

Don't Do It!

Never use automated lead follow-up or automated mailings on media contacts. They get more information than they want or need. Anything you send should be personalized and specific to the media contact's preferences.

Send Follow-Up Information

Reporters get bombarded with pitch letters and interview requests all day long, so the more personalized the information you provide them, the more likely it is to be read. Always reference previous conversations, such as any you had at the show, comment on articles they have recently written, and offer to be a resource for market information.

Any follow-up information you send should be limited to whatever the media contact is interested in. Don't send a huge packet covering every nook and cranny of your products and services. Focus on building a relationship that will enable you to introduce additional products at a later time.

Track Communications

As with sales leads, you want to track every communication you have with your media contacts. Aim to collect as much information as possible to help build a relationship with these VIPs. Not only do you want to track items and communications specific to your company and products, you also want personal information such as anniversaries, birth dates, the names of their children, or their favorite foods, all of which can help build a relationship.

There are specific PR tools such as Vocus, which already has a lot of that information about reporters available, plus you can add any information you learn. These solutions are not inexpensive, however, and often exceed budgets. If your company uses a CRM system, it might have a PR module already. If you have to resort to something more basic, Microsoft Outlook with Business Contacts Manager can be used quite efficiently.

Show Smarts

If your company has a CRM system but that system doesn't have a PR module, ask to get a "PR business unit" that you can use as a framework to manage all PR contacts and activity.

Track Media Coverage

It is important to track media coverage for a variety of reasons, including the third-party validation you can use for quotes and marketing materials. Some publications send you a copy of a magazine or sometimes just the article covering your product, but that is rare, and you don't want to count on it.

Ideally, you need to track both online and print coverage. The only practical way to do this is to utilize a clipping agency. A clipping agency is a company that specializes in clipping media coverage from both print media and online coverage, providing you with a weekly or monthly overview of your coverage. It's next to impossible to track print coverage without the help of such a service, but if you have to do it without spending that kind of money, sign up for search-engine-based alerts such as Google Alerts for automated keyword alerts. This enables you to track all of your online coverage.

The Least You Need to Know

- All leads and media contacts need to be managed by a central system such as a database or a customer relationship management program.

- All communications with your leads and media contacts need to be tracked and documented for future reference and to use for future follow-up strategy.

- Follow-up material sent to your most important leads, as well as media contacts, should be personalized and as targeted as possible.

- The use of automated marketing and lead follow-up tools can be good for a large spectrum of leads, but it should be avoided for the most important prospects and all media contacts.

- Contact all high-scoring leads within 7 days of the show closing and all other leads within 10 days of the show.

- Track media coverage to use for marketing material and to use as third-party validation.

Chapter 20

Postshow Exhibit Strategy Analysis

In This Chapter

- ◆ Learn to create an effective postshow report
- ◆ Identify what worked and what didn't
- ◆ Evaluate your return on objectives (ROO)
- ◆ Calculate your return on investment (ROI)

Now that you are back from your show, have gotten a little bit of rest, and have had a chance to recover, it is time to start working on the postshow analysis. While I hope you had fun at the show, the reason you went to exhibit was not to have fun but to meet the goals you previously set. Now you have to build a scorecard and see how the event did.

Evaluating results and performance is crucial to making improvements for future shows. Whether you decide to go to different shows or tackle the same one differently, the postshow analysis is what helps you make that determination. The post-show report is not meant as a finger-pointing or blame-storming exercise but as a tool to capture return on objectives (ROO) and measure return on investment (ROI). This chapter guides you through the common items that should be part of your postshow report, but you should customize it based on the goals you set for this particular show.

Marketing Approaches

At each show, you invest in several marketing approaches. This section of your analysis covers how each approach fared and how it contributed to your overall goal.

The CD provides you with a questionnaire to examine your exhibit strategy postshow.

Promotional Items

Describe each promotional item you selected and the messaging used on it. The actual value of each promotional item to the marketing activities is hard, if not impossible, to measure unless you happen to have seen them all in garbage containers outside the hall. It's more likely that attendees took them home, and from then on you have no idea what happened to them. What you can measure, however, is the willingness of attendees to be qualified to get one. If the item was popular and people were willing to go through a qualification process to get it, the item was successful regardless of what happens to it after the show.

> **Show Smarts**
>
> If you had multiple promotional items, you can calculate their direct value to the qualification process. Most of the time, you will find that several items were equally effective. Note the cheapest one for the next event.

Advertising Effectiveness and Entertainment Effectiveness

Advertising effectiveness is often a little easier to measure. Evaluate each ad or ad campaign you ran; if you had a call to action, describe how and if it was followed. Common means to measure the success of ads are to have dedicated phone numbers that are specific to a campaign, special "order codes" published only on specific ads, and defined web URLs. You can also ask about ads during your qualification process on the show floor.

If you had entertainment at your booth, such as a magician or just an entertaining presenter, try to evaluate its effectiveness in helping to reach the goals you had set. Normally this involves judging if the entertainment held the attendees' attention during a presentation or if it helped to get qualified attendees onto the show floor. Describe the reaction the audience had toward the presenter or entertainer.

Preshow Marketing Effectiveness and Marketing Improvements

Preshow marketing can be accurately evaluated as part of your qualification process during the show. If you ask attendees whether they saw any preshow ads or other material and if it influenced their decision to visit the booth, you have good data. You can then correlate that with your actual qualification data and get a picture of each activity's effectiveness. Describe each activity, its goals, and if they were met.

Write a couple of sentences about the marketing areas you want to improve. Even if everything went smoothly, you will probably be able to think of a few things to improve.

Other Marketing Approaches Discovered at the Show

During the show, you probably saw marketing approaches used by other companies that you had not seen before or previously thought of. Plagiarism is a type of flattery, so describe any new marketing approaches you discovered that might be worth emulating and compare them with the effectiveness of your own programs. It might be worth noting the top five marketing approaches you observed and creating a wish list of things you'd like to try yourself. That way you will have additional starting points for your next trade-show plan.

Booth Staff

Depending on the size of your company, booth staffers might largely be the same from show to show or might vary greatly. Either way, you should evaluate their effectiveness for every show, and areas for improvement need to be identified for the next booth staff training. At the same time, areas where the booth staff did well also should be noted.

Number of Booth Staff

One factor that requires continual evaluation is the booth staff size. Note the booth size and describe how booth staffers were able to deal with the traffic. Did each staffer have enough time to take breaks and reenergize? Was everyone able to attend the daily show meetings? Did sales have too many scheduled meetings to properly cover booth duties? Conclude with your recommendations for future shows.

Training Effectiveness

Provide an executive summary–style description of what was covered in your preshow training and then detail how well booth staffers followed the instructions given. Note the areas that need more focus in the next round of training and if a different presenter could help improve the training.

You should have a pretty good understanding of the booth staff's ability to answer the questions of prospects. Without naming individuals, note if there were booth staffers who needed a large amount of assistance from other team members.

Also make a top 10 list of questions that attendees were asking and make sure they are covered in any future preshow training and booth staff manual you develop. Of course, you can have more than 10 questions if you deem it necessary.

Rate the effectiveness of the training provided, note any areas that could use improvement, and explain how such an improvement could be achieved.

Show Smarts

Sometimes it is difficult to get your booth staffers to be professional during the role role-play part of your training sessions. If you feel that training needs improvement, consider bringing in an outside person. Your employees will react quite differently to an outsider.

Sales Meetings at the Show

Depending on when you write your postshow report (it should be fairly close to the end of the show), you may not know the true outcome of any sales meetings that were set up. Depending on the sales cycles of your products and services, sometimes you cannot wait to write the report until all sales results are in.

What you can measure and evaluate is how many meetings were set up and how many were actually held. In most sales organizations, a sales pipeline is grouped into various confidence levels that a sale will occur. If your sales cycles are too long to have actual billed revenue by the time you write your report, describe how those sales meetings affected confidence in the salesperson's ability to close the client and get the business.

Booth and Display Messaging

When you look at evaluating the booth itself, layout and display messaging are the two most important factors. For obvious reasons, there is only so much you can do with a 10'×10' booth.

We'll cover the layout questions shortly; for now, describe how the display messaging and graphics contributed to attracting attendees to the booth and if it was attracting the right kind of attendees. Were they prospects that would qualify in the lead process?

Booth Location

Describe the location of the booth. If you have an electronic copy of the show floor map, maybe insert the part that shows where your booth was located. Explain why the location was chosen and if the assumptions used in selecting the location turned out to be correct.

Explain what you liked and disliked about the booth location and how that might affect future booth location selection. If you feel your booth was in a poor location based on availability by the time you registered, be sure to register earlier next time if you want to exhibit at the same show again. Registering earlier typically also means greater discounts.

Booth Traffic

The booth traffic evaluation should cover the overall traffic the booth received, what percentage of visitors went through the lead-qualification process, and what percentage of visitors ended up being qualified leads. Explain if the booth was sized appropriately for the traffic it received and what size would be recommended should you choose to exhibit at this show again. Also describe how the layout supported an attendee's visit through multiple stations, or if the layout caused issues (such as areas that were too crowded or underutilized).

Improvements for the Booth and Messaging

Even if you followed all the tips and guidelines of this book, it's not impossible that you may have noticed some messaging on the show floor that you found particularly well worded or appealing. Don't be afraid to learn from good ideas you see and incorporate them into your own trade show planning. Make any recommendations you have for improving the booth and its messaging.

Lead Collection, Handling, and Analysis

Describe the lead process and how effective you feel it was. Pay special attention to the questions that were asked as part of lead capturing and how they helped with follow-up. List any additional questions that should have been asked and questions where the answers didn't help as much as expected.

In addition to evaluating the results, evaluate how practical the lead-gathering process was for both booth staffers and attendees. Also note if there were problems with attendees not wanting to answer specific questions.

Summarize the lead-scoring process and how well it performed in separating the leads by quality. If you performed lead scoring at the show, how time-consuming was that process, and did it interfere with other business-related activities that booth staffers would have done had it not been for this task? Evaluate whether other lead-scoring methods, like right after the collection of the lead, would possibly work better. Explain how well the lead-scoring process was understood by all booth staffers and if additional training is required. Conclude with any recommendations you may have on improving the lead-scoring process for the next show.

Show Smarts

Ask all team members for their input regarding the lead process. Get answers from all parties involved, starting with the booth staffers that collect the leads, and include the team members scoring the leads, the individuals submitting the leads to the office, as well as the staff in the office that deals with them once they come in. Ask what they found effective and efficient and where they see need for improvements.

Return on Objectives (ROO)

This section is about achieving objectives that are not directly sales-related items. These are activities and "customer touch points" that may contribute to accelerating a sales cycle, result in competitive information, or include media activities. List the goals in each area you had set and if and how they were met. Some of this information might already have been covered or at least been touched on in the section that covers marketing approaches. ROO is important, and you should repeat information here if needed.

Primary Objectives Accomplished and Not Accomplished

List each objective and describe your analysis of all the activities that led to accomplishing it. To illustrate this, let's assume one of your objectives was to get the media to cover your products and services. In this example, you might have distributed a press release over a newswire, directly contacted 20 reporters, left 30 press kits in the press room, and secured 10 meetings.

The results were that 25 press kits were taken from the press room, 4 articles were published referencing your products (make sure to list the publications), and 3 reporters followed up postshow to talk to your PR person. List these examples as the accomplishments for this objective.

It's important to take pride in what you accomplished, but it is no less important to identify objectives that were not met and why not. Sometimes you will find that the objective was simply not attainable because it was based on false assumptions, but failure might also be the result of poor planning or poor execution of a plan.

Identify the objectives that were not met and describe what was done to achieve them, where you think there was a breakdown, and how things could be improved at the next event.

Example of an Objective Not Met

Let's say one of your goals was to collect customer research on a product; prospects were to fill in an in-booth survey after the booth staff collected their lead information. There was an additional promotional item given to attendees who handed in their surveys. The objective was to collect at least 100 surveys, but you only ended up with 16 completed forms. Now you need to come up with conclusions for why this happened and improvements for next time.

The booth staff might have been too focused on collecting sales leads, for example, and neither booth staff nor attendees had the time to deal with the surveys. You may also find that the promotional item wasn't enough of an incentive, or you may find that booth staffers just weren't motivated enough to push the survey. Your findings should be followed up by a conclusion and recommendation. You may decide that this objective simply was a bad idea and shouldn't be an objective at a future show, or you may have concrete ideas as to how it can be achieved next time.

Improvements in Setting Objectives

You may have realized that too many objectives were set or that some of them were conflicting. For example, you might have had an objective to have each booth staffer talk to at least 20 attendees per hour, but you also had the objective of getting your research survey filled in. Booth staffers might have been faced with a choice of either reaching their traffic goal or reaching the survey goal. Check every one of your goals for conflicts with other goals you set; see what external factors have influenced your ability to reach your goals and how this will affect setting goals for your next event.

 On Chapter 20 of the CD, you will find a spreadsheet to report both your ROO and your ROI (discussed in the next section).

Return on Investment (ROI)

Ultimately, your ROI is what makes trade shows a viable marketing activity, at least it should be. The ROI is measurable and quantifiable. It is determined by comparing the total cost of exhibiting with the total revenue generated.

If you are in an industry with long sales cycles, this might be a lengthy process and can stretch over years. In that case, incremental or maybe quarterly updates are a good way of tracking ROI. In any case, you should have some ROI estimates based on where you are in the sales cycle. With a little experience, those estimates will typically be within 10 percent of your final results.

Number of Leads Collected

One thing you should be able to report within hours of the show closing is the number of leads collected. You should also break this down into the various qualification scores you defined. Leads should also indicate a timeframe of when the prospect is looking to make a purchasing decision. Depending on how far out that is, make sure leads (where appropriate) are given not only to sales but also to marketing for direct mail and similar campaigns.

Number of Qualified Leads Collected

The number of qualified leads collected is a number much more meaningful to the bottom line of your trade show exhibiting. Anyone can get a large number of leads by handing out T-shirts in exchange for swiping a badge. If you do that, you will have lots of leads and lots of frustrated salespeople who call huge numbers of attendees only to find out they don't care about your products but like your sense of fashion.

In the meantime, prospects who might buy your product are hidden somewhere in the lead pile. Qualified leads mean that the prospect has indicated a match between his needs and your products and has the intention of making a purchase decision soon. Those are the leads that need following up as soon as possible and are an important number to report.

Purchasing Timeframe

Create a table that shows your leads corresponding with a purchasing timeframe. The timeframe question in your lead-qualification process will depend a lot on the type of product you're offering, but it should always be a part of the qualification process. If you choose to use a table, what time span this should cover depends on the length of your sales cycles. Most tables will be in monthly or quarterly increments.

Number of Sales Closed

The ROI is determined based on dollar figures, while this category simply lists the number of sales closed. Like the ROI, this number might not be available quickly based on your sales cycles. Every time you update your ROI numbers, you should also update the sales number.

The reason both of these numbers are important is because the combination of the two allows you to draw conclusions with regard to the value of the audience you reached. It allows you to find the ideal trade show targets by identifying the revenue-per-sale ratio based on different shows and lead-generation costs.

Quality of Attendees

Compare the attendees with what was advertised in the show prospectus, and note any discrepancies between what you expected and what you actually saw. The quality of attendees from your perspective might have been higher or lower than expected. Quality is subjective; the audience that visited your booth might be perfectly suitable for your product, but because you expected and prepared for a different attendee profile, your results might not be as good as they could have been.

Competitors

We discussed competitors in Chapter 14, and part of your report should include what competitors were at the same show and how they positioned their products. Include their booth size and marketing activities. Make recommendations to position yourself better against your competitors; it is likely that they will use the same display and marketing approaches at the next event.

Actual Costs Versus Budget

This section of the report compares the actual costs with the budget for the show. It's possible to have stellar ROI results but also to have spent double what you planned to spend. This section is designed to identify possible errors or false assumptions in the budgeting process. If you were over budget, most likely you will have to figure out what to cut to stay within budget next time. If you have exceeded your show goals, you might get a budget increase.

Shipping Process

This section covers the entire shipping process, though the focus is on the performance of the carrier(s) you used. Evaluate the shipping company based on ease of use (such as the ability to track shipments online, 24-hour customer service, etc.) as well as shipping performance. Did the shipper pick up and deliver as promised? Were any items damaged or missing? Note specific dislikes and likes.

Travel and Hotel Arrangements

When you look back at travel and hotel arrangements, the key areas to focus on are how well travelers were informed about the selection of flights and hotels, how well they worked out, and what improvements could be made. For example, you may find that a hotel closer to the exhibition could have saved substantial time spent going back and forth or that many booth staffers missed the preshow meetings because of flight arrivals that were timed too tight. As always, if you have any recommendations for improvements, use them to conclude this section.

Determining Whether to Exhibit Again

When this is all written and done, it boils down to the big question of whether to exhibit again. In most cases, this refers to a specific show or audience. But in the most extreme case, it could literally be about exhibiting again at all. Ideally, collectively with other decision makers, you will evaluate the ROI and ROO with those from other trade shows and other marketing approaches for the same target audience. You may find that trade show exhibiting has a good ROI for your target audience X, while direct mail or a call center campaign works better for audience Y. Your report should conclude with a recommendation and any additional information that may affect the list of trade shows you are considering exhibiting at.

The Least You Need to Know

- You need to evaluate all aspects of your trade show experience to identify areas for improvement.
- Identify your ROO and ROI to measure the success of the show.
- Determine how you performed against your budget.
- Use the resulting data to decide whether you should exhibit at this show again or if other marketing vehicles are more effective.

Part 6

Special Types of Trade Shows and Activities

There are a couple of loose ends to tie up and things to discuss that were only touched on earlier in the book. Both table top exhibiting and international exhibiting are sufficiently different from conventional trade shows to deserve being mentioned separately. Many of the items from the previous parts apply, of course, but there are special things you need to know before participating in either type of show.

Finally, for good measure, we need to talk about what you can do when you are not exhibiting at all but are attending a show as a regular attendee. There are ways to improve your general experience, but there are also a couple of things you can do that will make you feel more like an exhibitor rather than just a visitor.

NICE TRY, FERGUSON... BUT I'M *STILL* **NOT** PUTTING YOU IN CHARGE OF OUR INTERNATIONAL TRADE SHOWS!

BARR

Chapter 21

International Exhibiting

In This Chapter

- ◆ Understand your motives for exhibiting abroad and what factors to consider when selecting potential countries

- ◆ Consider language barriers and common translating mistakes

- ◆ Trade show concepts are different and more relationship-focused than in the United States

- ◆ Learn international shipping rules and regulations

- ◆ Heed travel advice for U.S. citizens

When you decide to exhibit internationally, you enter an often completely different world. The moment you leave the continent or go south of the U.S. border, a lot of rules change. There are plenty of similarities, and the core concepts of trade show exhibiting all apply, but everything you do now has to be compatible with local customs and requirements. There are the obvious differences such as language and culture, but there are also more subtle ones such as trade show setup style, attire, or the booths themselves, which are usually called stands. You have to deal with the metric system, different electrical plugs and voltage, visas, import regulations, and other fun things that make this a memorable experience.

There isn't a one-size-fits-all list of differences between international exhibiting and domestic trade show participation. You have to learn the specific differences for each country you exhibit in. Learn as much as possible about the country and region's culture you exhibit in so that you don't look like an uncultured American.

Although you need to learn about the local culture and the most effective methods to reach prospects in each particular country you exhibit in, this chapter focuses on exhibiting in order to introduce your company or product to a new market. If you already have established operations or a distributor in an international region, you probably want your local teams to worry about the trade show rather than doing it yourself.

Benefits of International Exhibiting

The reasons for exhibiting abroad vary greatly, as do the benefits. The most common reason for exhibiting in a different country is to introduce your product or company. The obvious benefit then is gaining access to markets that you currently don't serve. Unless you are in the business of making only American flags, there are many more international prospects for your product than domestic ones.

While your primary goal might be finding international customers, be on the lookout for regional partners that can help with regional distribution, marketing, and support.

Many international trade shows are aimed at higher-level attendees than domestic ones, and it is common to sign and announce bigger deals during these trade shows. In general, there is a much bigger focus on building business relationships than individual sales at most of the shows.

Discovering unknown competitors and finding new ideas you can implement in your domestic products are two more benefits to international exhibiting. Because the U.S. dollar is relatively weak against most international currencies these days, now is a good time to expand your business internationally because your products and goods will be relatively inexpensive for foreign buyers.

Selecting a Country to Exhibit In

There are about 245 countries in the world, and at the time of this writing, there are 192 member states of the United Nations. Consequently, you need to spent some time thinking about what countries are worthwhile to exhibit in. As usual in the business world, this decision boils down to expected ROI, which in turn depends on a couple of factors you have to balance against each other.

Market Size

How big is the potential number of prospects for your product? Remember, count only prospects who can afford your product. For example, agricultural equipment is desperately needed in many developing nations, but farmers often cut grass by hand because tractors are too expensive for them, not because manufacturers decided not to sell them there. When determining the market size, also keep in mind cultural differences. For example, in several Asian countries the penetration of telephone answering machines is very low, so you might think that this is a good market for voicemail—until you discover that it is considered rude to leave voicemails and not answer phones in person.

Language

While there are more Germans than there are Brits and both have an identical need for your product, you may decide that going after the smaller market in Great Britain makes more sense because you won't have to worry as much about language issues. Sure, you may have to check your marketing material and make sure it doesn't use words that are too American for our friends across the Atlantic. But that task is nothing compared to translating everything into German. Also you might be able to get a United Kingdom telephone number forwarded to your office here so that you can provide sales and phone support. The moment you enter a market with a different language, you also have to worry about support, usage agreements, and many more things that are language specific.

> **Don't Do It!**
>
> Don't keep your existing product names without checking other possible meanings in a different language. For example, Rolls Royce was a little surprised about the reaction its new model, Silver Mist, received in Germany. Then somebody pointed out that the word "mist" means "manure" in German.

Legal/Regulatory Issues

Just because your product meets a need in a specific country doesn't mean you will actually be allowed to sell it there. Especially electronics and chemical products have very different approval processes. Research those well in advance of exhibiting there.

> **Show Smarts**
>
> Several countries accept foreign approvals from a specific economic region. For example, almost all products—with the exception of some pharmaceuticals—that are approved in one European Union country can be sold in all European Union countries. So if you want to enter the Spanish market, you don't necessarily have to go through certification in Spanish but rather get your certification in Ireland or Great Britain, where you can do the process in English.

Competition

You need to research local competition. It can be very hard to replace a strong incumbent, and you might be better off focusing on a smaller market where you have less of an uphill battle against a dominant competitor.

Comparing U.S. and International Shows

Remember, international trade shows tend to attract higher-level attendees and serve as a venue for high-level meetings and major contract negotiations. Visitors spend significantly more time in the stands, often creating the need for private meeting and hospitality areas. The following lists outline some of the most common differences between exhibiting in the United States and abroad. They are only glimpses, though, and this is by no means a comprehensive description of the differences.

def•i•ni•tion

A **shell scheme** typically consists of lightweight panels, a diagonal grid of ceiling beams, fascia panels on the open sides, and a name board with the exhibitor's name. The entry-level booth size is comparable to a 10'×10' booth.

U.S. Shows

- No technical testing of products by the show organizer.

- Pipe and drape booths.

- Material handling provided.

- Trade shows have seminars or an educational component.

- Custom booths can be built preshow and shipped to the show.

- Booths are planned to attract prospects to discuss their product needs, provide demonstrations, and gather leads.

- Attire is typically shirts with the company logo.

- Have fire codes but are not very strict.

- Shows are typically two to four days.

- Shows average four to six hours per day.

International Shows

- Many countries require product testing to ensure standards compliance before products can be exhibited.

- *Shell schemes* are the standard booths.

- No material handling provided.

- Most shows are exhibits only.

- Custom stands are often built on-site for a one-time use and are often referred to as a "build and burn" booth.

- Many stands set meetings in advance with prospects and have built meeting rooms; the focus is more on building relationships.

- Attire is expected to be conservative business suits.

- Fire standards are very strict, and many countries require certificates that certain items meet standards.

- Shows are typically four to five days; others last up to two weeks.

- Shows average eight hours per day.

Rules and Regulations

Just like back home, exhibit regulations vary greatly depending on location, as do ceiling heights, floor load capacities, and general layouts. Because relationship building has a higher importance at international shows, booths are usually more enclosed or at least have some enclosed areas for private meetings, and most inline booths have side walls. Frequently, booth designs must be submitted to the show organizer for approval regardless of size, height, or location in the exhibition hall.

In many countries, regulations covering the use of fireproof or fire-resistant materials are much more stringent, particularly in Japan and Europe. Expect an ever-present fire marshal during the installation phase who may conduct actual fire tests using a lighter. In France, for example, Plexiglas is not allowed at all because it releases toxic fumes when it burns. Other countries such as Germany require fire extinguishers in all two-story booths.

Many countries have specific and much more stringent environmental policies, so you should factor in much higher cost for certain services such as waste disposal. As at home, it is important to know all the rules and regulations.

Planning Timeline

Six months is a safe timeline for planning for an international exhibition. Of course, this depends on the size of the booth as well as whether you have exhibited in that country before and already have appropriate materials and gained local experience.

If this is your first international show or your first show in a particular country, you may need more time to plan. It takes considerable time to learn a foreign exhibiting process as well as to select and effectively train the appropriate staff. Since attendees will want to deal with people on their level, expect to have executive-level staff in your booth, which may further complicate your planning timelines.

Key Things to Understand About Your Booth

You need to pay attention to a lot of nitty-gritty details about your booth, such as electrical considerations, what type of booth display to use, who constructs your exhibit, measurement conversions, and fire standards.

You should also plan to focus much more on building relationships with attendees versus gathering leads. Keep in mind that, if you don't already have a presence there, you may not be taken seriously in this market until you have participated in several shows. Focus on finding local business partners and distributors, not end customers, during your initial exhibiting.

Exhibit Space and Measurement Conversion

Most countries outside the United States use the metric system of measurement. When you design your display, keep in mind that international shows don't use pipe and drape and that booth space sizes vary widely. Remember also that exhibits are frequently custom built in the show hall and used only once.

Booth space is typically purchased by the square meter, which makes it easier and cheaper to get space that matches your booth needs. Most the time, a shell scheme is used for entry-level booths. This option enables you to inexpensively add banners and materials or a small portable display. Make sure it fits first.

Electrical Differences

Your electrical needs vary greatly by country; there is no international standard. Always check what type of adaptors and transformers you need to bring to run your equipment and whether the equipment will even work with the adaptor. Also not every transformer complies. Electricity is either alternating current (AC) or direct current (DC). Frequency is either 50 or 60 hertz (Hz) or cycles per second. Voltage also varies; there are 12 types of attachment plugs in use around the world, with several countries using more than one type. Laptops and cell phones typically work with the right adapter. Lighting is especially troublesome when the voltage or frequency is different. You are usually better off renting lighting locally.

> **Show Smarts**
>
> Many electrical items (such as desktop computers, monitors, and projectors) have a switch that enables you to change the power supply to a different voltage. Check your equipment before buying transformers or renting equipment.

Sitting and Socializing Areas

If the space you have purchased is large enough, plan to have a seating area where staffers can sit with attendees. You should also consider having beverages available. In some countries, it is more common to offer alcoholic beverages rather than sodas or water. Check what is customary before planning this approach.

Display and Graphics Considerations

Messaging rules are consistent no matter where you are—you want to advertise your product's benefits and attract attendees to the booth. If you need to translate booth messages into the local language, use a well-respected localization company that uses native speakers. Even perfectly translated text can sound funny or may have a double meaning if it isn't checked by a native speaker. If necessary, ask for suggestions and consider alternative messaging that is better suited for the cultural environment. Be conscious of the graphics you use as well, and understand the significance and meaning of any symbols and colors you are considering using.

Significance of Numbers in Some Countries

Your exhibiting is about numbers, primarily the ROI. But it is critical to know and understand that numbers are important in certain cultures for other reasons. For example, the 2008 Olympics opened on the 8th of August at 8 P.M. Why? Because 8 is considered a lucky number; the Chinese word for "8" sounds very similar to the word that means "prosper." In contrast, the numbers 4, 5, 6, and 7 are considered unlucky. Every culture has its own sets of lucky and unlucky numbers. You don't want to have a product version or booth number that means something like "death" to the local population.

Booth Installation and Dismantling

As you are used to hearing, these rules also differ from country to country. Many countries do not have unionized labor, and some do not offer services that require skilled labor at all. The display house that provides your exhibit typically provides or contracts necessary labor, including any for hanging graphics and connecting electrical outlets as well as for lights and plumbing within the booth space.

Because booths are usually more complex and require more time to build and get certified, trade show move-in and setup times are longer—typically a week. Work ethics vary; people usually work at their own pace and take time out for tea breaks, naps, or even beer breaks. Guard against attempting to speed up the process because that may only result in a rebellion against the pushy Americans.

While tools and methods may be different from what we are accustomed to in the United States, in the end the job always gets done.

Key Cultural and Etiquette Items

If your staffers do not speak the local language, you may need to hire translators. In many countries, English is spoken enough that this might not be necessary; in others, English is not spoken at all. Consequently, the number of translators you hire depends on booth size and your target country. All staffers should familiarize themselves with several words and basic phrases in the local language, for example: "Hello," "Good-bye," "Please," "Thank you," "Nice to meet you," and so on. Making an effort is considered polite and is typically well received.

When entertaining clients or business partners in local restaurants, expect the food to be different from what you are used to. Be polite and eat what is offered to you if the local person orders for the group.

Local Business Etiquette

When doing business, take the time to learn about the importance and significance of appearance, behavior, and communications. The key to building successful business relationships is to be respectful and sensitive to each country's customs and the way business deals are handled.

The following are several important items you should research for each country you exhibit in. Keep in mind that this is only a list of examples; additional research on business etiquette specific to each country is suggested.

 ◆ If the local language is not written in roman letters, have bilingual business cards printed with English on one side and the local script on the other side. In addition, professionally translate all necessary collateral items.

 ◆ Understand how to present the business card. Some countries have a high respect for business cards and take pride in the way they are presented to one another. Also, writing on business cards is often seen as offensive.

 ◆ Use titles when addressing people. In very few countries is it normal to use first names. Instead, use Mr., Mrs., Miss, Professor, Doctor, and so on. In some countries, it is common to address people by only their professional title.

◆ Understand how timing works in each country. Some are strict about punctuality, while others are typically late.

◆ Know what is acceptable gift giving and at what stage in the relationship-building process it is appropriate.

Local Businesses' Decision-Making Process

Be aware that negotiation styles are very different abroad and that many may seem rather absurd to us. Body language can be an important part as can personal space. Also, the actual decision-making process varies greatly by country. Some cultures are very "top-heavy," while in other cultures decisions get "recommended up" from very low-level employees through various level to an actual decision maker. I know I start to sound a little like a broken record, but be sure to research the local customs.

Shipping Logistics

International shipping is more difficult and frequently quite expensive, especially when using air freight. Shipping things across an ocean takes time and requires a fair amount of advance planning. You need additional documentation, which is critical to getting your items through customs. Forms might have to be completed in languages other than English, and some countries require you to pay import fees even if the exhibit is exported following the show. Shipping costs are the main reason why building an exhibit locally tends to be more economical. Expect at least three to four weeks of shipping time for ground or water shipping and seven to ten days for air.

Customs Documents

An experienced freight forwarder with links to local customs services can tell you what documents are required. The following is a list of commonly required customs documents:

◆ **ATA Carnet:** This is a something like a travel document for shipping goods issued by the United States Council for International Business (USCIB; www.uscib.org). The ATA Carnet demonstrates to customs officials that you are bringing in the merchandise only temporarily, as is the case for a trade show display.

Show Smarts

While not required, an ATA Carnet is accepted in more than 50 countries and is valid for one year. It can make your shipping much easier. Beware of high penalties, however, if you fail to export the items after the show.

♦ **Temporary importation under bond (TIB):** If you don't use an ATA Carnet, you have to post a bond to guarantee that the merchandise will be exported.

♦ **Certificate of origin:** This document, required by some countries, states where the items in the shipment were manufactured, not where you are exporting them from.

♦ **Temporary export license:** This is a specialized license required by the U.S. government for the export of products that could affect national security, such as arms, aircraft parts, and certain high-tech equipment. Licenses are issued by either the Department of Commerce or the Department of State.

Shipping Documents

In addition to customs items, you also need shipping documents:

♦ **Commercial invoice:** This is a list of all items being shipped (including exhibit booths) with their dimensions, weight, and value. Anything you plan to export back should be listed using the manufacturing value, not any resale value.

♦ **Packing list:** This list of items in each package must be accurate and specific. "Exhibit materials" won't cut it. There is no official form for either the commercial invoice or the packing list. A commercial invoice and packing list are almost always required and might be needed in both English and the local language.

◆ **Shipper's export declaration:** This form is required by the
Department of Commerce for some shipments valued over $2,500.
It is completed by the freight forwarder. If you use an ATA Carnet,
the USCIB, which issues the Carnet, can provide the necessary
forms.

Freight Forwarders

Freight forwarders transport your shipment to the port airport and
normally help with any necessary documentation. International exhibit
freight is more expensive but provides additional services such as deliv-
ering to the booth, unpacking, storing empty crates during the show,
and finally getting everything back to where you shipped it from.

Customs Brokers

A customs broker receives goods at the destination, declares the value
of the shipment, and processes the paperwork. It also usually handles
the payment of any required fees. While you can pick your own freight
forwarder and customs broker, it makes sense to use an international
freight forwarder and have it contract with the customs broker to avoid
any delays.

Typical Travel Documents for U.S. Citizens

Since 9/11, a passport is required for all travel outside of the United
States. You can still walk across a couple of bridges to Canada with just
your driver's license and a birth certificate, but the moment you board
a plane, a passport is a requirement. Always check whether a visa is
required. Some countries allow entry without one for certain lengths of
stay. Some countries require you to have a visa before arriving in that
country. It is always a good precautionary measure to register with the
U.S. Embassy or Consulate in the country you visit so that it is aware
of your presence in the country. You can do this online. In the event of
a family emergency in the United States or a local disturbance, it can
contact you and help if necessary.

Don't Do It!

If you need a business visa to exhibit at a trade show, don't try to get around it by using a tourist visa. Depending on the country and its laws, you might be fined, jailed, and/or deported.

The Least You Need to Know

- If you decide to exhibit internationally, consider more than just the market potential of your product. Also keep in mind costs for translating your material or getting local certification.

- Avoid common translation mistakes and always use native speakers for localization jobs.

- Negotiating and decision making may work quite differently than back home; make sure to research local customs in advance.

- Make sure you understand all local requirements such as environmental or safety regulations before ordering your booth space.

- Shipping material internationally is a complex and time-consuming process; make sure you plan for enough time.

Chapter 22

Table Top Exhibiting

In This Chapter

- The different types of table top shows available
- Table top strategies for various opportunities
- Different table top displays
- How to find table top show listings
- Planning a table top event and the time you need

A table top show is by far the cheapest way to participate in something resembling a trade show. Your "exhibit area" is usually only a skirted 8' or 10' table. These shows are much different from the average show you will go to; the typical exhibitor at these shows is extremely inexperienced in exhibiting. Now, I realize that is a rather blunt statement, but it's true! You will find that the infamous "fish-bowl" technique is commonplace. It's a sure way to collect a lot of business cards, which of course nobody knows what to do with after the show. If you use that method, please go back to Chapter 13 before continuing on.

Let me tell you a quick story that humorously proves my point. I once walked through a table top expo and saw a booth decorated like a Halloween supply store, complete with costumed booth staff in clown suits handing out candy. It had cobwebs, skeletons, spiders, the works! It was around Halloween, so I assumed they sold Halloween costumes and asked where their store was located. They laughed and said, "We're not a Halloween store, we're CPAs, isn't this so fun?" I took a close look at the booth again to see if there was any hidden hint that they were CPAs instead of Halloween store owners. I couldn't find one—no signage or collateral, just business cards and candy. I have to admit I did smile—in amazement, though, not because of the clowns. I don't know about you, but a CPA that dresses as a clown is not getting my business, that's for sure!

So as you can see, a tiny bit of exhibiting knowledge gives you a huge advantage at these shows. If all you do is buy this book and read nothing else but this chapter, you already belong to the top 10 percent of exhibitors at most table top shows! And you can easily make the top 1 percent by reading a few more chapters.

Common Table Top Exhibiting Shows

Table top shows are most frequently organized by chambers of commerce or associations. Occasionally, large companies offer table top shows as part of a bigger event. Table tops are also offered—although rarely—in a designated area within a regional or national show.

There are exceptions, but most of the time table top shows are not targeted. Your biggest benefit is increased exposure among the other members of the chamber or association that organizes the event.

Show Smarts _____

Use table top shows to educate the other members about your business and products. Focus on showing them how to refer business to you. Trying to collect leads and "selling" attendees on your products and services is mostly wasted time.

Chambers of Commerce

Almost every chamber of commerce organizes at least one table top show per year. Exhibitors are members, as are most of the attendees, though you can expect other members of the community such as local businesses to attend. Normally these shows last three to four hours, but in the case of very large chambers, they can be an entire day. Typically those events are held in the ballroom of a local hotel. Promotion of these shows is often limited to some flyers, newsletters, and maybe an ad or two in local newspapers. Sometimes they are listed in the calendar section.

Don't Do It!

Often you see gimmicks being sold to exhibitors that are meant to attract attendees to your booth. For example, exhibitors may pay to be part of a treasure hunt. Attendees are encouraged to visit all display tables, and when they do, exhibitors stamp their treasure hunt card. At the end of the show, attendees who visited all booths on the card receive a prize of some sort.

Stay away from purchasing these gimmicks. It is money wasted on people who only want their cards stamped. They are not qualified visitors. The game reduces your opportunities to meet with qualified prospects. You are much better off focusing on your signage and marketing materials to draw qualified attendees to your display table instead. (See Chapter 8 for more information on messaging.)

Associations

Industry associations organize table top expos primarily as part of regional events managed by a regional chapter. The "parent association" usually organizes an annual, traditional trade show with pipe and drape booth spaces as well as educational offerings.

In most cases, a table top expo organized by an association includes seminars and other educational programs that are covered in the following sections. Table top expos organized by associations are otherwise very similar to the ones managed by chambers of commerce, but they tend to be held in more upscale locations. The environment is typically more educational and informative, and attendees might be reasonable prospects. Since most attendees come intending to learn, promotional items with some educational value, such as a little booklet with industry tips, are a great way to be remembered—better than another rubber ball or hat that gets passed on to friends and family.

Seminar Add-Ons

Many associations (and the occasional chamber of commerce) offer educational seminars, round table discussions, and panels as part of an educational program. A table top expo is often designed as an environment where attendees can take a break during sessions, or the table top area is used for a networking event. Those table top expos can have pretty good results, especially when the educational sessions cover areas that fit your products or services because that means attendees are more likely to match your target profile.

If possible, look for opportunities where you can be part of the educational program. For example, as a speaker, you can establish yourself as an expert in your field. Normally you are not allowed to promote your company or products during those sessions, but you can certainly answer any follow-up questions later and tell attendees where to find you. You can also offer to demonstrate solutions to the issues discussed in your seminar at your display table or use your products as examples during your session. It's a fine line to walk, but during the session your primary mission is to be a likeable, knowledgeable expert, not a salesperson.

Show Smarts

Associations are always in need of new educational topics to present to members. Take advantage of this opportunity by finding the appropriate person to hear your pitch for a seminar topic that has not been presented to the association before. This is primarily something that only members are allowed to do, but occasionally presentation pitches are accepted from an outside expert.

If the association accepts your pitch, it will often create an entire program around the educational topic, with table top exhibiting opportunities, networking, and so on. Ask if you are entitled to a complimentary display table; if not, purchase one to maximize the opportunity and exposure.

Designated Area at Larger Shows

Finding a table top area at a bigger show is rare, but it does happen. While this might look like a great opportunity to participate in a bigger, often more targeted event, it has a downside. Your validity may be questioned because it appears—true or not—that you can't afford an actual booth space. There is risk that your company will be perceived as a "wannabe" that isn't quite ready yet. I don't recommend that domestic companies exhibit in these situations. I have, however, seen foreign companies exhibit successfully in these areas because, in the eyes of attendees, the expectations for those companies are different because of the distance they traveled to be part of the show.

Business Partner Events

Business partner table top expos are my personal favorite when it comes to table top exhibiting. They are often organized by a large business that either sells your products or vice versa. Another possible partnership is when one of you has a product complementing or requiring the other. These expos are usually inexpensive, if not free, for exhibitors. The upside is that the larger company has a motivation to make you more successful and give you an opportunity to showcase your product.

Attendees are typically the larger business's other business partners, current customers, local prospects, and often some local media. These events are a great place to find targeted leads. You should always consider an offer to participate in one. Treat these events as you would a traditional trade show: plan well, create goals, train staff, and focus on engaging, qualifying, and collecting lead data from attendees. In these situations, you probably need to go with the paper-based lead form or Card Scan® Lead Qualifier to collect lead information.

Finding Exhibiting Opportunities

Table top expos are harder to find using the more conventional methods discussed in the first chapter of this book. Chambers of commerce newsletters or their websites are often the only sources for finding chamber events. They do get limited coverage in local newspapers, but at that point it's often too late to exhibit. The same thing holds true for table top shows of regional industry association chapters, though those tend to be scheduled farther in advance and are almost always listed on the association's website as well as promoted in e-mails to members.

The method for selecting partners to participate in these types of expos varies greatly and ranges from "any partner is invited" to sales- or revenue-based criteria. In almost all cases, the organizer has some discretion as to who gets invited to participate. If you know one or more of your partners are organizing this type of event, keep asking your contacts what you have to do to participate; odds are you'll be invited. If not, you should at least learn what the criteria are for next time.

Typical Table Pricing

Of course, pricing varies depending on the show. Some partner events may be free, while others cost a few hundred dollars for a regular table. There are also regional differences, and the same association may have different pricing in different cities because the venue costs are higher.

Preshow Planning Timeline

Admittedly, you need a little less time planning for a table top expo than you do for a traditional trade show, but you still want to make sure your business looks professional. Give yourself at least two to three months if you have a display and up to four if you need to design and acquire a display. There are far fewer details to worry about than with a traditional show, but you still need a solid strategy to maximize the return on the money and time you spend.

Show Smarts _____

Create a planning timeline and master planning guide to keep track of all tasks, just as you would for a traditional trade show. You can customize the master planning list on the CD so that it is appropriate for your table top exhibiting needs. Also use the budget planner to track costs and determine ROI from the show.

Similarities with Traditional Exhibit Opportunities

We've talked a lot about the unique aspects of table top exhibiting, and while there are many differences, there are also many similarities.

Just like their big brothers, table top expos provide an opportunity to showcase products and services to other businesses that can be potential prospects or recruited for referrals.

You still need a lead-gathering process, though in most cases the paper form is the clear choice. You may want to have promotional items to help with lead qualification. Booth staff training is very similar, too. While it shouldn't take a long time to explain where items are located on your display table, qualifying techniques and other booth protocol items apply here as well.

Differences from Traditional Exhibiting Opportunities

There are a couple obvious differences such as the shorter show times and the simple fact that you have less space available. Of course, there are fewer services offered than at a big trade show, but there are also a couple of less obvious differences that may result in a problem if not considered in advance. The first is that you cannot count on electricity being provided unless it is specifically stated. If you plan to show a presentation, make sure you have enough laptop batteries to last during the show times.

Show Smarts

If you would like to run a presentation but have no power or not enough battery time on your laptop, consider buying a battery-powered digital picture frame and upload each slide as a picture. Because these devices have no hard drive and generate little heat in comparison to a computer, the batteries last much longer.

Cautions for Table Top Exhibiting

When considering whether to exhibit at a table top show, be conscious of who the show organizer is. If the organizer is new at this, be prepared for few attendees or, conversely, completely overcrowded aisles. Planning a table top event properly is much more difficult than you might think, and many event organizers and their exhibitors learn that the hard way.

Often a chamber or association decides to organize a table top event because it sounds like a good idea. It doesn't give much thought to attendees, targets, traffic flow, and show facilities. Before registering as an exhibitor, ask questions about how the group intends to promote the event, what the show floor diagram looks like, and similar questions. If you hear statements such as "We will be promoting the event everywhere" or "Everyone will be there," be cautious. That doesn't sound like a well-thought-out strategy!

Table Top Display Options

Even though you don't have a huge amount of space, there are plenty of creative products that can turn the surface of a table into a small trade show booth. Messaging on your display is the most important component, and all the rules and ideas from Chapter 8 apply here as well. Pricing for professional table top displays ranges from about $300 to $1,500, though of course it's possible to find a way to spend more. If you are considering exhibiting at multiple table top shows, spending the money on a higher-end display is worth it.

Table Top Pop-Up

Table top pop-up displays are pretty much miniature versions of pop-up displays for regular 10'×10' booths; they're simply designed to fit on top of a table. Like their cousins found in traditional booths, they come with various frame types and may have wrap-around fabric for a finished look. Because they are small enough to fit on a table, they are easily transported, and many of them fit within airline carry-on requirements, simplifying the setup process. You arrive at the show, put your frame on the table, pop it up, attach the printed panels (often made with Velcro), and you are done setting up your display. The downside to these displays is that they need a lot of space on the table, often leaving very limited space for lead forms, a demonstration laptop, and marketing material.

Panel Systems

Panel displays are popular at table top shows, probably because of their low cost. Essentially they are fabric-covered panels that can be printed or used to support signage. Unfortunately, they often look dated or cheap—more like a science fair project than a professional exhibit.

Briefcases

There is a display type that is somewhat similar to a panel system except it folds up to the size of a briefcase, making it really easy to carry. The panels are also fabric, and graphics and signage are attached with Velcro. While more practical to move around than conventional panel systems, the outcome often looks just as homegrown.

Banner Stands

Banner stands are a good display option because they are fairly cheap and can be reused at all kinds of events, including bigger booths. The type that works best is the double-sided banner stand with telescoping height. Have your banners printed at 24"×36" as described in Chapter 8.

Using a double-sided banner stand creates signage that can be seen walking down the aisle from either direction and leaves your table free for marketing material, lead forms, and demonstration space. You can fit these stands right against the table where they take up no space or violate anybody else's display space.

Sign Holders

Use basic sign holders, such as those you find in any office supply store, to provide additional signage with specific *call to action* information. They are very inexpensive and complement any of the other display types.

def•i•ni•tion

> A **call to action** tells prospects what you want them to do. At a show, you may want an attendee to ask you a question, request a certain item, and so on. In a show advertisement, your call to action would be "Visit us at display table [number]."

Collateral

Your collateral choice should be the same for a table top show as for any other show that attracts a similar audience. It is important that attendees leave with additional information about your company and your products. Chapter 10 covers collateral items in greater detail.

Show Smarts

If you are participating at a table top show hoping to recruit other businesses for referrals, bring enough collateral to give to companies that are willing to work with you.

The Least You Need to Know

◆ Don't expect table top expos from local chambers or associations to attract a lot of targeted attendees. Focus on educating friendly businesses about what you do and work on recruiting referral contacts.

◆ Table top shows that are part of a bigger trade show or a partner event should be treated like traditional shows with target prospects and regular lead collection.

◆ Multiple display types are available for table top shows. Have concise messaging and avoid creating the look and feel of a science fair project.

◆ You need the same type of collateral that you would bring to a bigger show. If you want to make contacts for referrals, you may even need more than at a conventional trade show.

Chapter 23

Optimizing Time as a Nonexhibitor

In This Chapter

- ◆ Schedule your time to maximize the benefits of attending a show
- ◆ Evaluate vendors and their product offerings
- ◆ Track and evaluate the show
- ◆ Go beyond just being an attendee

There might be many reasons you decide to attend a show. In many cases, you want to learn about products and services you are considering for your company. Attending may also be a cheaper alternative to exhibiting if your objective is to connect with existing customers or select prospects, since those activities don't necessarily require you to have your own exhibit.

The focus of this chapter is maximizing the benefits you get out of a trade show from a pure attendee perspective. You need to bring enough business cards and have some collateral of your products with you. However, be aware that many shows have so-called "suitcasing policies" and may ask you to leave if you are overly aggressive about promoting your own products.

Create an Attendance and Product Budget

Before you do anything else, figure out what you want or can afford to spend on attending the show. If you are attending to evaluate products you might purchase, you should know your budget for that as well.

As far as the attendance budget goes, make sure to factor in all seminars, travel costs, and expenses for activities with media or clients. You can use a similar approach to the one used in Chapter 3 to create a trade show budget. If you are required to get approval to visit a show, creating a set budget and defined goals will make the approval process easier and will increase your chances of success to get to the show and while at the show.

Hotel Discounts for Room Blocks

Always look for the show hotel discounts. Often you can get to a reservations link directly from the show's website. Savings can be substantial, and show hotels are either in walking distance or will provide a free shuttle service.

 Show Smarts

Often several hotels are in a similar price range within the same distance to the show. Some of these hotels will probably host networking events you plan on attending. Staying in the same hotel will save you time and money.

Conference Packages

Most shows will not only offer a variety of conference packages, they often make them available at substantial discounts if they are purchased by a specific deadline. Make sure you know what those deadlines are to take advantage of those early registration rates if you can make your decision early enough.

Planning Before the Show

Whether you exhibit or just attend, planning is key to your success. The following sections discuss the tasks you should complete before the show.

Review the Website

Planning starts with the show's website. It contains valuable information such as exhibitor lists and booth locations, networking events, and seminars.

You may receive additional invitations to exhibitor-sponsored events in the mail or at booths during the show. The majority of your preshow planning and scheduling, however, will be based on the information found on the show's website. Armed with information about exhibitors and events, you can start planning your time at the show.

Plan Your Schedule Before the Show and Review Seminar Offerings

Take a calendar and mark the timeframe you will be in the show's city. Mark the actual show hours in a different color and start filling in the available time with exhibitors you want to see and seminars you want to attend.

Entering the items that have fixed schedules first, such as seminars or networking events, will make it possible to get the most out of the time you have available. Next schedule any prearranged meetings and fill the remaining time with exhibits you plan to visit.

If part of your reason for going to the event is seminars and sessions, look at the schedule on the show's website. It is not uncommon for sessions to get added at the last minute, so keep checking back.

> **Don't Do It!**
>
> Don't add items to your calendar based on what comes to mind first. Add items with a fixed date and time first and add the most flexible items last.

Register for the Show

After you have decided on a list of seminars and sessions you want to attend, look for the right package that allows you to attend the sessions you are interested in without having to pay for the ones you are not.

Also, if you are certain you will be going to a show, make use of the early registration discounts. They can be considerable and will leave you with more of a budget for other things like hotel choices. Registration is usually available online, but sometimes you are required to fax information with a signature. In most cases, a credit card is required at the time of signup and usually gets charged at that time.

Review Exhibitors and Products

If you are attending to learn more about products, whether you are looking to buy or do competitive research, you should download the exhibitor list from the show's site if it is available. Typically these lists include product categories, making it easy to sort by those categories and to identify vendors of interest.

Creating Attendance Goals

Writing down goals for the show will help you stay focused and allow you to better evaluate the success of your visit, improving your productivity at the next show you visit.

You should set goals for areas such as number of vendor booths visited, number of vendor meetings prearranged, number of media appointments scheduled, and number of networking events attended. You may want to have a networking plan similar to the one discussed in Chapter 19.

List Target Vendors and Booth Numbers

After you have made your list of vendors, print a map of the exhibit hall and mark the booths you plan to visit. Determine how much time you think you will need at each booth and then start scheduling your booth visits based on location because that is the most time-efficient way. There is no point in crossing the entire exhibit hall 10 times to see 10 vendors. Make a list with each vendor's name, the time allocated, and the booth number.

Preschedule Vendor Appointments

You will probably have a couple of "must see" vendors, as well as others that you are simply interested in but certainly won't be upset if you don't see them. I recommend prearranging meeting times with the ones that are important to you. This ensures that the appropriate members of the vendor's staff will be available, and you'll spend less time waiting around for someone suitable to deal with your questions and needs.

Review Networking Opportunities: Create a Plan

Just like every booth staffer needs to create a networking plan for every show (as discussed in Chapter 9), you should also have one as an attendee. As a matter of fact, you should not only have one, but one for every networking event you attend. This doesn't have to be a 10-page document. Your own personal bullet points are probably enough, but you should have a plan and goals to avoid wasting time.

Show-sponsored events are listed on the show's website and should be easy to find. Also be on the lookout for postal or e-mail invitations you may receive in the weeks leading up to the show. Sometimes you will receive an invitation to a booth you want to visit. You might have to sacrifice another scheduled activity if you deem the newly available opportunity more important.

Pitch Attending Media

Just because you are not exhibiting doesn't mean you can't have press meetings while you are at the show. Press meetings rarely happen at a booth anyway; they tend to occur over breakfast, in the press room, or in other meeting rooms. So if public relations are part of your job or your company otherwise trusts you in this capacity, there are many PR activities you can do as an attendee.

Getting access to the media list without being an exhibitor is the biggest challenge. Media attendees are rarely listed on a show's website. While it never hurts to call the show producer and ask for the list, especially if you mention you are considering an exhibit, I wouldn't count on obtaining it. If a business partner of yours is exhibiting, you might be able to get the list from him or her. Otherwise, you will likely have to look at last year's media coverage to get an idea as to which publications are likely to cover the event.

When you contact reporters to set up appointments, be prepared to talk about a new product or have a list of upcoming articles from their editorial calendars that you think you might be able to help with. Media members get pitched all day long, and their primary reason for being at the show is to report on things at the show. Because you are an attendee, your primary angle should be to position yourself as an industry expert who can help them understand the industry and market better.

Bringing Employees and Colleagues

There are a couple of reasons why you may want to bring a co-worker to the show, and I am referring to reasons that will benefit the company. The first and most obvious one is that there might simply be too much ground to cover for a single person. This is particularly true if the event has many good and valuable seminars. Seminars and sessions typically run in multiple tracks, and it's impossible to be in three to six sessions at the same time. Sometimes you can get a DVD of the sessions; otherwise, if you want the information of more than one session, you have to send more than one person.

Trade shows can be a great opportunity for junior staff members to learn about the industry, the competition, and networking events in a compressed timeframe. Needless to say, if you are considering having more than one person attend, make sure this fits into the budget and get approval if necessary before asking anyone to join you.

Attire

Dress codes vary from show to show, and while you might be only there to attend seminars or check out vendors, you should always try to make a professional impression. This becomes even more important if you are doing media meetings or networking events. Business casual is probably fine for most occasions, but you may want to consider a suit if wearing one is common in your industry.

The most important clothing is your left and right shoes. You will walk and stand a lot during the show, and comfortable yet professional-looking shoes are highly recommended. After three days in uncomfortable shoes on a show floor, you'd be willing to pay any price to get comfortable ones and to get rid of your blisters. Be smart and deal with that problem upfront. I have a pair of shoes that

Don't Do It!

Dressing professionally is important. Most shows aren't fashion shows, so don't dress in a way that becomes uncomfortable. Discomfort can easily distract from your primary tasks at the show. Nobody wants to walk around the floor sweating or with hurting feet.

I exclusively wear at trade shows; I call them my trade show shoes, and they have saved me from a lot suffering over the years.

Arriving at the Show

When you arrive at the show, you will most likely have to pick up your attendee badge first. Even if you have been mailed one, you will probably have to activate it. You may need ID to get your badge, and you will typically receive a bag with a lot of stuff in it, ranging from pens to collateral and CDs. Many of the items in your bag are probably useless, but it often contains invitations to networking evenings or updates to schedules, so make sure you don't throw those out.

Press Kits in the Press Room

If you are planning to do PR activities, be sure to leave a couple of press kits in the press room. Don't forget to include your cell phone number because you won't be able to direct anyone to a booth. You may get turned away trying to enter the media room because you don't have an exhibitor badge. If you don't know a media person who can help you get in, hold your cell phone to your ear, look like you are going to meet someone and are already late, and chances are nobody will stop you.

Bring a Bag for Carrying Information

Notice how many attendees hold a plastic bag in their arms because it got too heavy and the handles ripped. If the show doesn't provide you with a good bag at registration, stop by the first booth that offers decent bags as a promo and get one. Otherwise, bring one of your own.

> **Show Smarts** _____
>
> If your primary mission is to collect a lot of collateral and other material, ask vendors if they can mail you material or bring a laptop bag with wheels and a handle so you don't have to carry tons of material across the trade show halls.

Bring Several Business Cards

One thing that always surprises me is the number of people who run out of business cards during a show. Bring at least three times as many as you think you may need. It is unprofessional not to have cards.

In the Exhibit Hall

If this is the first trade show you are attending, be prepared to have your senses overloaded with sounds, colors, lights, signs, speeches, and crowds of people. Exhibitors try anything imaginable to get you into their booth, so schedule some down time to recover and relax.

Guiding Vendor Booth Conversations and Meetings

As previously suggested, you should have a set schedule with a fixed time you are willing to stay at a specific booth. You may have to take charge of your conversations and keep booth staffers focused on your questions and needs rather than allowing them to ramble on about whatever they find great about their products or their company. Always keep in mind you are there to be productive.

Products: Take Notes and Pictures

Bring a notepad to take notes. With all the things going on at a show, do not expect to remember details by the end of the day. It's also a good idea to have a digital camera to take pictures of things that are of interest to you, though you should ask for permission before taking any.

Disengaging from Unqualified Vendors

While a good booth staffer should qualify you, you also have to qualify the vendor. If you conclude that a particular vendor is not able to meet your needs, it's time to stop wasting your time and their time and move on. Just politely disengage from your conversation and move on to the next booth on your list. Chapter 9 has for more detailed disengagement techniques.

Show Specials: Purchasing or Ordering

If you are in the market for a solution and are looking to make a decision based on the things you learn during the show, ask vendors for show specials. If allowed by the show, many will offer incentives and discounts for orders received during the show.

Don't Do It!

Be mindful of your budget. Hanging out at vendor booths offering solutions outside your budget can be fun, but in the end only wastes your time.

Visit Competitor Booths and Gather Information

Even if you are at the show for completely different reasons, never waste an opportunity to check out your competitors. Ask questions along the lines of what was discussed in Chapter 17 to gather information that will help with your product positioning and marketing.

After the Show

Create a postshow report based on the notes and information you collect. Cover all areas such as vendor evaluations, product evaluations, networking events, and media meetings as applicable.

Use your narrowed-down list of possible solution vendors to come to a purchasing decision within the purchasing framework of your organization.

Once you have prepared your post-show report, use it for the following activities:

- Evaluate if you met your goals by comparing your results with the goals you set before the show.

- Determine how to adjust or improve your goals and scheduling for the next event.

- Determine your future attendance based on if the exhibitors have met your company's needs and the quality of the sessions you attended. If you achieved your goals and think you are likely to have the same or similar goals again, it probably makes sense to attend that show again.

- If you haven't made a purchasing decision or order during the show, follow up with the vendors that made your hot list. All sorts of vendors will follow up with you, so make sure to let the eliminated vendors know you will not be using them. It will save you and them a lot of time otherwise wasted in additional follow-up calls.

Finally, make sure you record all expenses for your expense report or for your tax return.

The Least You Need to Know

- Set a budget to attend the show and get approval if required.

- Create goals and schedule your activities during the show to optimize the use of your time and maximize opportunities.

- Don't miss opportunities to meet with media just because you are not exhibiting.

- Register for expos and seminars early to benefit from discounts and to secure your place in sessions.

- Have a networking plan outlining the events and the contacts you want to make.

Glossary

air ride   A shock system found in trailers. It allows for a smoother ride with less bumping around of freight.

assets   Sometimes called fixed assets, an accounting term for items that are the result of a one-time transaction and that provide a benefit for an extended period of time, normally the lifetime of the asset. For example, you may buy a company truck once, but the company benefits from it as long as the truck remains in service.

benefits   How your product helps the customer.

bill of lading   A commercial shipping document that establishes a contract between the exhibitor and the freight company. It also serves as a receipt and includes shipping charges, a description of pickup and drop-off locations, freight check-in deadlines at the show, the number of items being transported, a description of packaging, and the weight of the shipment.

brand management   The application of certain marketing techniques to increase perceived value of a specific product or product line.

business-to-business (B2B) shows   Events where both attendees and exhibitors are all businesses.

C-level executive   A top-ranking person within a company. (Chapter 1 outlines the individual C-level executive titles.)

certificate of liability insurance   Evidence of the financial capability of a company to compensate for damage or loss incurred by its actions.

certificate of origin   This document, required by some countries, states where the items in the shipment were manufactured, not where you are exporting them from.

commercial invoice   A list of all items being shipped (including exhibit booths) with their dimensions, weight, and manufacturing value.

common carrier   An inexpensive transportation option with longer and bumpier transits.

consignee   The shipping term for the person or entity receiving a shipment.

conversion   The process of converting an initial lead into a sale. Sometimes called "lead conversion."

customer relationship management (CRM)   A process implemented by a business to handle all its contacts with customers and prospects. In most cases, a software solution is implemented to support this process. Software can store customer information, prospects, sales leads, and so on.

customers   The entities buying your product.

decision makers   The individuals making the purchasing decision for a customer.

depreciation   An accounting term that describes the spreading of the cost of an asset over multiple years.

drayage company   Essentially the material handling company at the show site. It manages all goods and freight entering and leaving a trade show.

enterprise   Often defined simply as Fortune 1000 companies.

features   What your product does and how it functions.

forced freight   A shipping issue resulting from problems with your material handling form, requiring the removal and shipment of your items by show services. This costs a significant premium.

freight forwarder   A company owning and operating some of its own trucks but also brokering shipments to partner carriers that can offer competitive prices.

gross weight   Sometimes called "heavy weight," this is the full weight of the freight truck including shipment. It is weighed upon check-in to the marshalling yard.

guerilla marketing   Marketing based on unconventional approaches used to promote and attract interest in a product or company using time and imagination as key components. Small- and medium-size companies find these approaches appealing.

large businesses   Companies with more than 500 employees.

light weight   The weight of the freight truck excluding the weight of the shipment after off-loading the shipment at the loading dock. It is weighed upon checkout from the marshalling yard.

loading dock   The area of the convention facility where freight is received and off-loaded before being delivered to the exhibitor's booth.

marshalling yard   The location designated by show services for freight carriers to report and be weighed before and after deliveries are off-loaded at the show site's loading dock. It also functions as a trailer staging area throughout the duration of a trade show.

medium-size business   A company with 101 to 500 employees.

messaging   Applied to a wide variety of marketing materials, it is basically just text communicating key points or action items you want the reader to do.

niche market shows   Shows for exhibitors of a subset of a larger industry.

packing list   An accurate, specific list of items in each package. There may be no official form for the list, and it might be needed in both English and the local language for international shows.

PRO number   The progressive numbering system used for tracking, billing, and identifying freight.

public sector   A category for your planning in addition to businesses.

receiving report   Written notification, completed at the loading dock, of the shipment being off-loaded. It documents that the shipment has been received and accepted by show services.

shell scheme   A booth with lightweight panels, a diagonal grid of ceiling beams, fascia panels on open sides, and a name board with the exhibitor name. Basically this is comparable to a 10'×10' booth.

shipper's export declaration   A form required by the Department of Commerce for some shipments valued over $2,500. It is completed by the freight forwarder and can be provided by the U.S. Council for International Business (USCIB), which issues the ATA Carnet.

show carrier   Usually a freight forwarder, it often provides show-specific services and show-specific discounts.

show services company   Contracted by and working with the show producer to create the show, it provides exhibitors with all information related to the show. Show services are ordered directly through this company, which provides show support before and at the show.

small business   Typically defined in North America as a company with 11 to 100 employees.

small office/home office   Typically businesses with 10 or fewer employees, often operated from a home.

temporary export license   A specialized license required by the U.S. government for export of products that could affect national security, such as arms, aircraft parts, and certain high-tech equipment. It is issued by either the Department of Commerce or the Department of State.

temporary importation under bond (TIB)   Guarantees that merchandise will be re-exported if absent ATA Carnet.

trade show producer   Sometimes called the "show producer" or "event organizer," this entity creates the idea, content, marketing, and promotion of the show; sells exhibit and attendance packages; selects target audiences; organizes educational seminars and networking events; and runs the show's website.

traffic flow   The direction or path you create in your booth layout, directing attendees through your exhibit space.

unique selling proposition (USP)   A description of your product's advantages over your competitor's product.

users   Individuals using your products.

van line   Higher-priced air-ride service, sometimes called a "white glove" service, it usually provides many additional services (pad-wrapping freight) that other carriers will not. It often requires third-party unloading labor.

vertical market shows   Shows for exhibitors with products that serve a particular industry such as insurance, healthcare, or legal.

Industry Resources

A list of trade show industry resources has been provided to further expand upon the content of this book. You will find where to directly search for trade shows, learn what industry associations and publications are available, and the reputable vendors I recommend (they have provided excellent service to clients of mine).

Trade Show Search Engines

- Trade Show News Network: www.tsnn.com
- Events Eye: www.eventseye.com
- Trade Show Calendar: www.thetradeshowcalendar.com/index.php?BNR=tsteacher
- Jupitermedia Events: www.jupitermedia.com
- All Conferences: www.allconferences.com

Industry Associations

- Center for Exhibition Industry Research: www.ceir.org
- Corporate Event Marketing Association: www.cemaonline.com

- Exhibit Designers and Producers Association: www.edpa.com

- Exhibitor Appointed Contractor Association: www.eaca.com

- Exhibition Services and Contractors Association: www.esca.org

- Healthcare Convention and Exhibitors Association: www.hcea.org

- International Association of Assembly Managers: www.iamm.org

- Destination Marketing Association International: www.destinationmarketing.org

- International Association of Exhibitions and Events: www.iaem.org

- Professional Convention Management Association: www.pcma.org

- Society of Independent Show Organizers: www.siso.org

- Trade Show Exhibitors Association: www.tsea.org

Industry Publications

- BizBash Media: www.bizbash.com

- Exhibit City News: www.exhibitcitynews.com

- Exhibitor Magazine: www.exhibitoronline.com

- EXPO Magazine: www.expoweb.com

- Destination Marketing: www.destinationmarketing.org

- Meetings and Conventions magazine: www.mcmag.com

- Penton Media, Inc: www.penton.com

- Primedia Business Magazines and Media: www.primemedia.com

- Tradeshow Week: www.tradeshowweek.com

Trade Show Vendors

Linda Musgrove, the TradeShow Teacher
E-mail: Linda@tsteacher.com
Phone: 1-888-547-7410
Website: www.tsteacher.com

Provides trade show training, educational products, templates, and resources.

Ben Nazario from MC-2
E-mail: ben1stern@yahoo.com and bnazario@mc-2.com
Phone: 609-548-0032
Website: www.mc-2.com

Provides information about custom-designed booths.

Ron or Greg Abbate at Expo Depot
E-mail: support@expodepot.com
Phone: 1-888-736-2490
Website: www.expodepot.com

A great resource for help and information about smaller displays, such as pop-ups, table tops, etc.

NMR Events
E-mail: jhogan@nmrevents.com
Phone: 609-433-2443
Website: www.nmrevents.com

Provides information about lighting and special events.

Frank Natoli from Global Events Management
E-mail: frankn@globaleventsmgmt.com
Phone: 305-345-7743
Website: www.globaleventsmgmt.com

A great resource for shipping and transportation information.

Appendix C

How to Use the CD

This book includes an easy-to-search CD that contains higher resolution images as well as a variety of templates that can be used and customized as part of your trade show preparations. As much as possible, templates are available in multiple file formats, but some of the templates do require Microsoft Excel 2000 or later.

To use this CD, you need the following:

- ◆ Equipment: PC or Mac with a minimum of 256 MB RAM

- ◆ Operating system: Windows 2000, Windows XP, Windows Vista, or Max OSX or higher

- ◆ Browser: Internet Explorer 6 or higher, Firefox 2 or higher, Safari 2 or higher

Contents of the CD include:

Chapter 1:

- ◆ Trade show search engine websites

Chapter 2:

- ◆ Template containing shows and key details

- ◆ Selecting shows to exhibit at questions

Chapter 3:

◆ Budget template spreadsheet

Chapter 4:

◆ Master planning checklist

◆ Planning meeting checklist

◆ Binder tabs for planning binder and where to place paperwork from the exhibitor kit

◆ Suggested supplies spreadsheet

◆ Suggested supplies spreadsheet—already filled in

Chapter 6:

◆ Various booth examples—color pictures

◆ Questions to ask when considering used displays

Chapter 8:

◆ Targeted design examples from two TradeShow Teacher clients

Chapter 9:

◆ Asking open-ended questions in the booth

◆ Disengaging from unqualified prospects

◆ "Booth crimes": bad booth behaviors to avoid

◆ Conversation starters and open-ended questions for networking

◆ Asking for referrals

Chapter 10:

◆ Setting goals and objectives

◆ Selecting marketing activities based on goals and objectives

Chapter 11:

◆ Press release template

Chapter 12:

◆ Characteristics of end users and customers

Chapter 13:

◆ Lead fulfillment planning

Chapter 14:

◆ Competitor analysis spreadsheet

◆ Competitor press release tracking sheet

Chapter 20:

◆ Postshow exhibit strategy analysis—booth staff to complete for each show

◆ Postshow ROI (return on investment) and ROO (return on objectives) spreadsheet

Index

T